Wild

Wild

Poems selected and edited by
Joan Fenney

Wild: Poems selected and edited by Joan Fenney
ISBN 978 1 76041 564 8
Copyright © poems individual authors 2018
Copyright © this collection Ginninderra Press 2018

First published 2018 by
Ginninderra Press
PO Box 3461 Port Adelaide 5015
www.ginninderrapress.com.au

Contents

Introduction	Joan Fenney	11
Rhythm of the Night	Helene Castles	15
The Wild Thread	Jude Aquilina	16
Calling to Wolves	Sharon Kernot	17
See My Feathered Fingers	Elaine Barker	18
The Vast Blue	Kathryn Riding	19
The maid (Cape Town in the 70s)	Maureen Mendelowitz	20
a dance	jenni nixon	21
Feral	Geoff Page	22
Uncontrolled	Maureen Mitson	23
In Spaces Between	Carolyn Masel	24
Brief Sketches of the Kelly Gang	Kevin Densley	25
The Rails	John Malone	26
The Utterances of a Child	Cassandra J. O'Loughlin	27
Diva From Budapest	Jennifer Chrystie	28
Dancing in the rain	Margitta Acker	29
Respecting the Wildlife	Melissa Bruce	30
Signs	Laurie Brady	31
Boxed-up Corners	Myra King	32
Untamed	Ann Simic	33
Advice to Girl on Leaving Home	Linda Albertson	34
Wild Janus	Betty McKenzie-Tubb	35
Red	Christopher Nailer	36
Five Hours Late	Jean McArthur	37
Freedom Fighter	Lisa Milner	38
Ride the Wind	Jennifer Sinclair	39
Captured	Janette Dadd	40
Jungle Predators	Kathy Abrahams	41
For Sasha Ruby, at 8 months	Ros Schulz	42
Fence Down	Philip Radmall	43
Y/our Dark	Anne Morgan	44

Carnal Spirits	Lyn McCredden	45
… and a new road	Janey Mac	46
Where else we can find history…	Linda Wells	47
Wild Bereavement	Elizabeth Goodsir	48
Maniots	Jill Nevile	49
Tamed?	Annette Jolly	50
In the Wilds of my Mind	Kristin Martin	51
Beach Walk, Binalong Bay	Graeme Hetherington	52
DNA	Margaret Bradstock	53
For My Son	Dorothy Hansen	54
It's an Emergency	Dominic Kirwan	55
Urban dis-ease	Rosemary Winderlich	56
Night Dreams	Mary Pomfret	57
A Wilderness	Melanie Duncan	58
My firstborn	Sam Duncan	59
Silver brumby	J V Birch	63
The Tyger	Joe Dolce	64
Warrigal	Gail Willems	65
'River Horse'	Shelda Rathmann	66
Wolf	Adriana Wood	67
All on a summer's day	Jane O'Sullivan	68
Stamped with the Caption	Hazel Hall	69
Under the panda cam	Judy Dally	70
Mother says	Alice Shore	71
On the Wolf Trail	Martin Jon Porter	72
Thylacinus cynocephalus	Sue Cartledge	73
Bomber's Moon	Margaret Collett	74
David Attenborough…	Zenda Vecchio	75
Natural Habitats	Edna Taylor	76
Because, like the weather	Russell Erwin	77
meerkat at a summer *milonga*	Avril Bradley	78
On the Daintree River	Mark Mahemoff	79
The Wildest Beast	Margaret Clark	80

Anjing Warrior	David Taylor	81
Not in the wild at all!	Margaret Bolton	82
Camping on the edge…	Russ Talbot	85
Night on Blackhorse Creek	Cary Hamlyn	86
on empty	John Carey	87
Wilderness was a sentence	Roland Leach	88
Brachina Gorge	Pam Morris	89
Kati Thanda-Lake Eyre	Gillian Telford	90
The Mountain's Song	Catharine Steinberg	91
Bush Tucker Tour	Brenda Saunders	92
Return to the Desert	Adrian Rogers	93
Excursion To Windjana Gorge	William Cotter	94
The Diamantina	Jack Oats	95
Mawson's Hut	Geoff Graetz	96
Desert Sand	Ian Coulls	97
Cradle Mountain	Fran Graham	98
Maralinga: Dead Country	Adrian Lane	99
imagining what you can't…	Sandra Renew	100
Four-wheel Drive Initiation	Sue Cook	101
En Route To Alaska	Moya Pacey	102
Entering the Forest…	Danny Gardner	103
The Black Snake	Ian McFarlane	107
From the Tree	Paul Williamson	108
Sanctuary	Tracey-Anne Forbes	109
Grasshopper	Ann Nadge	110
tree creeper	Rob Walker	111
Galahs	Gordon McPherson	112
Wildlife in the City	Airlie Jane Kirkham	113
Every Frog Has His Day	Robert M. Steley	114
Avian	Maggie Slattery	115
The Dark Side of Nature	Barbara Gurney	116
Other Species	Lorna Thrift Brooks	117

Like Thistledown	Jacqui Merckenschlager	118
fingers	Ashley Capes	119
Mollymauk	David Harris	120
caged	Colleen Keating	121
Animal Attraction	Michele Fermanis-Winward	122
Why we shouldn't trust birds	Christopher Palmer	123
Dunbogan	Paul Cliff	124
Scarlet Robin	Maurits Zwankhuizen	125
Fishy Secrets	Carolyn Cordon	126
The Albatross	Ray Clift	127
Tamed by Love	Jean Winter	128
Wind	John Egan	131
At Reedy Creek	Suzanne Edgar	132
Flood Proof	Helga Jermy	133
A Womb of Trees	Anne Collins	134
My Cliff Face Self	Diana Bell Brooks	135
The Lambing, Night Watch	Peter Hansen	136
paranoid wind	Tim Metcalf	137
meteor shower	Fiona McIlroy	138
silence…	Jacqueline Lonsdale Cuerton	139
When winter winds blow	Jill Gloyne	140
Rainforest Fungi At Dusk	Max Merckenschlager	141
Beyond the Tree of Heaven	Robyn Mathison	142
January seafarers	Adèle Ogiér Jones	143
Undersong	Irene Wilkie	144
As Summer Comes	Julie Thorndyke	145
of gales and zephyrs	Jacqueline Buswell	146
underbelly	Kathleen Bleakley	147
Considering Fred Williams…	Barbara Fisher	148
Sunday At the Lake	Amelia Fielden	149
A murmuration	Chris Hall	150
The moon is in its place…	ML Grace	151
Flexing	Brenda Eldridge	152

Winter	Angela Johnson	153
Antipodes	Jane Carmody	154
moreton bay fig	Kevin Gillam	155
Rough Sea Journey	Jill Gower	156
Gum Saplings	Jayne Linke	157
Paterson's Curse	Jena Woodhouse	158
Winter Beach	Rose Helen Mitchell	159
Close your eyes	Jeff A. Harbrow	160
The Ancient Guardians	Jen Gibson	161
Telling the Wild Wood Story	Jan Norman	162
Different Every time	Peter Frankis	163
Lone tree silhouette	Greg Tome	164
Winter Storm Front	Thérèse Corfiatis	165
The Weight of Water	J. Richard Wrigley	166
Invasion	Mary Jones	169
The black one	Louise Nicholas	170
A matter of perspective	Valerie Volk	171
Flux	PS Cottier	172
Spoken Words	Gabrielle Journey Jones	173
Moonlit Beauty	Susan Fitzgerald	174
Riparian Zone	Magdalena Ball	175
Bronte Beach	Libby Sommer	176
Free within the Cage	Anthony J. Langford	177
Stampede	Dianne Kennedy	178
Safety in numbers	Rodney Williams	179
Old Vinyl Anger	Martin Christmas	180
The Lie	Andrew Drake	181
Water World	John Watson	182
The Kettle Boils	Antony Fawcus	183
A Holy Night…	Rebecca Kylie Law	184
Exit from the City	Jules Leigh Koch	185
Afterword	Stephen Matthews	186

Introduction

'The mind that finds its way to wild places is the poet's…'
Gilbert K. Chesterton

At the heart of every poet is a wildness to create – a braveness to put their innermost thoughts on paper. With a blank piece of paper, the poet goes into uncharted territory – to imagine, to venture, to let words run wild. As Vincent Van Gogh said about the creative process, it is about letting go 'without limits'.

Ginninderra Press poets from around Australia responded in overwhelming numbers to the challenge of submitting poems on the theme of 'wild'. The poets whose work was selected unleashed their creativity and imagination to produce poems that covered a gamut of subject matter and themes. From a child dancing 'the moon alight' to 'the wild thread of love'; from the silver brumby 'hunted for the moon in his coat' to the currawong 'wolf-black with white flashes'; from 'the black heart of scrub' to the wilds of 'The Diamantina'; from a house riding 'on wind waves' to the 'feral beasts' of music and poetry – contributors illustrated what Henry David Thoreau said: 'This world is but canvas to our imaginations.'

The nature of 'wildness' has been depicted in songs, films, books and poems. Songwriters, scriptwriters, novelists, non-fiction writers and poets have explored 'wild' in relation to people, places, nature, animals and small creatures. From songs – 'Born to be Wild' to 'Wild Horses'; to films – *Wild at Heart* to *The Wild Bunch*; to books – *The Call of the Wild* to *The Wild Geese*; to poems such as 'The Wild Swans at Coole' by William Butler Yeats – the concept of 'wild' captures the writer's imagination. It is the sense of the untamed, the passionate, the fierce and impetuous in our world that fascinates us – often a world that is the antithesis of our own. Ginninderra Press poets have brought their originality to the fore to explore their own meaning of the concept of 'wild'.

Wild is GP's sixth anthology since the press's inception in 1996. Publisher Stephen Matthews initiated the anthologies to give Ginninderra Press writers further opportunities to publish their work, and as he stated 'they have been successful in creating a sense of community among the writers'.

Previous anthologies have explored themes relating to Port Adelaide; artist Hans Heysen and his home, The Cedars; what writers collect; and social justice. Stephen has taken this latest Ginninderra Press anthology in a bold new direction with the theme of 'wild'. He stated that this theme allows for a broad interpretation and 'gives a huge scope for contributors to explore'.

The launch of the *Wild* anthology is part of the celebrations to mark the tenth anniversary of Ginninderra Press's successful relocation from Canberra to Adelaide. Thank you to Stephen Matthews and Brenda Eldridge of Ginninderra Press, and to all the poets who have contributed with enthusiasm to this anthology. The poems in this collection illustrate, as Linda J. Wolff wrote, 'Even the wildest of ideas can come to mind. If we only learn how to imagine.'

Joan Fenney

'I want movement, not a calm course of existence.
I want excitement and danger and the chance to
sacrifice myself for my love…'

Leo Tolstoy

Rhythm of the Night

I saw a child who danced the moon alight
arms outstretched in moving shadows deep
with rhapsody she danced   secure in the rhythm of the night.

The miners and the monuments   the stars that shimmer bright
she spread her arms to feel   to gather in   to sweep
I saw a child who danced the moon alight.

The enigma glows   the dancer slows   in time the two ignite
the desert winds rush in   embers of her soul to reap
with rhapsody she danced   secure in the rhythm of the night.

Her mood   her feet   her face   portray an act of pure delight
the outback clay-pan firm and warm receives her joyful leap
I saw a child who danced the moon alight.

Hunting creatures hesitate   confounded by the sight
she pauses   closing eyelids   miming images of sleep
with rhapsody she danced   secure in the rhythm of the night.

The impact builds   a riddle solved   delivers then takes flight
a vision so intense that it may not be mine to keep
I saw a child who danced the moon alight
with rhapsody she danced   secure in the rhythm of the night.

Helene Castles

Previously published in *tamba*, Issue 59

The Wild Thread

The texture of love is loosely woven
and cannot be knitted from a pattern
it's smooth and elusive as water over slippery rock
it is crystal-studded, yet soft to touch,
bright as moss or cornflowers before a storm.

The texture of love is Braille – to be read aloud softly
with two hands clasped together like a solved puzzle.
The wild thread of love is tissue thin, yet resilient,
strong and bonding as cobwebs,
its silver thread glistens and sings on the wind.

Jude Aquilina

Calling to Wolves

For Oliver

Some days he's wide awake, his eyes sparking,
his ears alert, his voice calling to wolves, or laughing.

There are seizures though, some small – petit mal – and others,
grand and wild, that chip away at his mind and at the time.

Time. This is what we have – time to think, time to ask
what the poet thinks, time to write it down.

We try to keep it light and so there are jokes.
What is the point of heaviness when your limbs
and your voice are already locked up?

This process, this poetry, is an unwrapping, a slow revealing
and a patient waiting and craving by the poet
who knows what he wants to say.

We, the scribes, are not always able to decipher his thoughts
from the hunches, the nods, the hand movements
but he guides us forwards, slowly.

There are surprises. There is depth, complexity, insight: profundity
as we unscramble scattered syntax and creative word play.

Poetic moments stretch to hours, to days, to weeks,
but he builds and we record his words – brick by word-brick –
waiting for a poem to emerge.

Sharon Kernot

See My Feathered Fingers

Someone said, 'If my body were a temple
you'd decorate the walls.'
My body is my temple, my dwelling place,
my skin's the canvas that stories me.
See the bleeding heart and crucifix here?
It's for my mother when I began.
This knife is twisting for my dad, the time
I did him in – a bit of luck, that,
which explains the horseshoe on my arm.
The book and candle's a clever thing.
The dragon stretching down my back
in crimson and black and gold,
its claws embedded in my skin,
cost me more than I can say.
With my tattoos I've come this far
to free myself, to belong.
There's lighter stuff as well.
See my feathered fingers, rainbow bum
and the snake down there's a nice surprise.
All my life is here and where I've been,
what I've become. Now you've seen me
as I am, enter my temple,
come right in. Kiss my painted lips,
feel my studded tongue.

Elaine Barker

The Vast Blue

In the rare air of Timbuktu they once again
tried to make sense of their troubled relationship.
She walks out into the soft clean air of the desert
the sand is silken under her feet
she feels as if an unseen force is moving her
as if she could go on forever
in the distance,
nestled before the shadows of a rippling erg
she sees a small Tuareg camp
blue men against golden sands beneath a rose sky
she has the sensation she might still be dreaming
one of the men is crouched next to a fire
fanning coals with a miniature velvet slipper
he offers her a thumb-sized glass of tea
the sugary sweet mint sends a message to her brain:
I love you and you love me, nothing else matters, nothing at all
when she returns they lie together and watch the moon
a fine white arc disappearing into the vast blue.

Kathryn Riding

The maid (Cape Town in the 70s)

I come into your home barefoot
With calloused soles of uncouth shape
And tramp the carpets of your stairs
The glass of tiles, the tiles of glass
The perfect smoothness of your feet
The narrow white of birdlike bones
I rub the glow and wipe the white
And gather some imagined dust
And think of dust storms I have known
And other storms of bubbled mud
And wind and wind and goddamned wind
That whines and curls through paper panes
And endless mould and endless rain
That cracks the mud that forms the pools
That drips and flows and won't be blocked
And causes cries and rising heat
In young in old until the cold
Succeeds the heat and larger holes
Are hacked and hued with
Baked hard hands
And hardened hearts at backyard graves
Do mark those graves with hard-baked stones
These hands of stones that smooth the sheets
That labour for a silken life
Of genteel breeze, of cut-glass rays –
A rainbow painted in the sky
You are serene   You do not know
My storms, my darkness, my desire
I smile your smile, I serve your tea
While dark does surge twixt you and me

Maureen Mendelowitz

a dance

as though climbing mount everest
he pulls at the bannister one step at a time
friends with everyone   loyal to none
voice in his head accuses   'you hold me back
could be someone by now'   his partner clings to his arm
they push on together toward the impending avalanche

her blonde wig askew   too thin for the frock
as if at a school formal leans for support from her beau
she's doing the slow soft-shoe shuffle with jack dancer
can she take her super early for the casket and plot?
he'd rather buy himself a boat   dreams dissolve into debt
he steals her pills   stoned on endone and methadone
spends nights cleaning   scrubbing away
smells and stains of her disease
helps shake out his fears   failing her
in their cosy cocoon they squabble and coo
like rainbow lorikeets looking for lice

her ashes in a heavy box from the funeral parlour
'she is the love of my life' he sobs
though not for long   the money's gone
on drugs to numb the pain   and booze
says he's over it now   doesn't need sex
spinning out of control   until the music stops

jenni nixon

Feral

Of course, one had to be elected,
sooner if not later.
And now they're swearing in their cheery
'pest exterminator'.

Confronting all his hazchems, they
are cockroaches in peril.
Equipped with spacesuit and a spray
he's certified as 'feral'.

Watching from the galleries,
we're more than half-elated
but, no, within an hour or two
it's plain he's been sedated.

Our 'feral pest exterminator'
hands in his mask and spray;
then settles back to grow his paunch
and take a rise in pay.

Geoff Page

Uncontrolled

Adonis recumbent
strapped to a gurney
innocent youth resplendent.
Blond curls black lashes
eyes closed against a world
he finds a challenge
at only seventeen.
Learning, yearning
hoping – not coping.

Snap! Eyes wide cerulean focus
shoulders arch, head tips
features distort, muscles fraught
lips curl, spit
emit 'Tina! Crystal! Ice!'
Thrashing, gnashing
writhing, scything
growling, howling
wetting, fouling.

Knees to his chest,
vomits, chokes, arrests.
CPR the doctor's skill
thumping, pressing
still. This parent, fraught, inept
her heart unable to accept
such beauteous youth reduced
by glistening shards of death
those sirens 'Crystal', 'Meth'.

Maureen Mitson

In Spaces Between

For Uncle Jack Charles

She sits meekly in the back,
ankles crossed,
hands clasped,
defying interference.

She has only to look out
to ride the cowcatcher
in front of the tram,
then the footboard, then

grab the passing car-door handle
with three fingers, and,
feet first, float her body
straight up like a kite

or spring from roof to roof
across the crumbling city,
hiding behind awnings,
sleeping by train lines,

quiet as dirt,
safe from all lassoing eyes –
they've not even caught a glimpse of her,
free as a cartwheeling windblown seed.

Carolyn Masel

Brief Sketches of Members of the Kelly Gang

Joe Byrne: balladeer, ladies' man,
spoke Cantonese (he needed
opium from the Chinese),
could hit a penny tossed into the air
with a rifle shot,
Ned's trusted second-in-command.

Steve Hart: ill-tempered,
sometime jockey,
had a mount that could jump the railway gates
at Wangaratta
– his claim to local fame.

Dan Kelly: clever, hawk-eyed,
destined to wear the passed-down clothes
of bigger, older brothers,
useful in a brawl.

Ned Kelly: proud,
crack marksman, fine boxer, trick rider,
addressed women with a parson's manners,
his *riastarthae* – alexandrite eyes,
born leader, fallen
on the law's wrong side.

Kevin Densley

Previously published in *Quadrant*, October 2007, and in *Vigorous Vernacular*, Picaro Press, 2008

The Rails

when I go off the rails
I'll eat strawberry flan and chocolate cheesecake
wear my slippers to the shopping mall
my pjs to the mail box
play my beethoven string quartets real loud like I did
my elvis records when I was fifteen
when I go off the rails I won't be nice to mr fydler
just because he's a senior
nor put the tv down when my kids ask me to
nor empty the dishwasher when
I don't eat home at night
when I go off the rails
I'll leave my newspapers just where I've read them
blare my horn all morning just to let my neighbours know
I've got one too
say what I really get up to when I 'go for a walk'
change my password on the internet so my brother-in-law
can't sneak on
and when I go off the rails
like tootle the train engine
chasing butterflies
in the meadow
I hope no one puts me
back on track
too soon

John Malone

The Utterances of a Child

For Claire

Surely the song larks on the Hay plains heard your call
on the landline, and the birds in the atolls of light
on the Murray. The bright-eyed quolls would have stopped
to listen in the mountain's deep-scented shade.
Certainly the koel in the fig would know it was you,
and the restless boobook that twirls curlicues in the fog.
Your breath to my senses is as the breeze to the bending grasses.
Rain falls on my face, on my hands, as I wait for your next call.
Your voice sends out light from every syllable, every vowel
and consonant…there is no one who can explain this.
The household words gathered in your four years are sweet
raspberries at my breakfast table, wrens on my pillow.

Cassandra J. O'Loughlin

Diva From Budapest

At first
he only had one word for her: languid
but then he found he couldn't stop
words spilling from his tongue
a treasure trove of ivory, of emerald
with amber tints

Sleeking hair behind her ear
she lounged, all nonchalance
half-hidden by bamboos and palms
her dappled coat inviting him
to stroke and stroke

The Danube rippled in gipsy eyes
pools of passion he dare not fathom
He felt her breath scorch his skin
her cloying perfume swamp his fear
of power coiled to spring

Then she yawned and stretched
in that loose-jointed feline way
shook jet lag from her shoulders
and purred at the crowd
of ecstatic fans

Jennifer Chrystie

Dancing in the rain

A long time ago,
when I was but a mere child
They called me the wild one,
And, boy, was I wild!

I clambered up mountains,
I jumped from the sky,
My mood wildly daring,
I lived on a high.

I danced in the sunshine,
I danced in the rain,
I danced with abandon,
Like I'd never be dancing again.

I plunged into oceans,
Rode wild waters so fast,
And sometimes, just sometimes, I wondered,
How long will this last?

It lasted a long time, but I am old now,
And lonely and no longer wild,
But dreaming forever of what I did
When I was but a mere child.

Margitta Acker

Respecting the Wildlife

My grandfather
just ran out
slowly.
He looked after himself so well
it took a long time
like a well kept car
not driven too often.
Looking good until the end
he wore a suit and tie
in his lounge chair
until his
lounge chair
wore him out.
My father called it
'a good innings'
the 91 years
possibly hoping for the same
but my father
drove everywhere,
'made' shall we say
'the most of his wheels'
and the parts
fell off
all over the place.
Dismissed at 84.
But when he was out
my brother and I
did nod and say
'Damn good innings!'
anyway.

Melissa Bruce

Signs

no sudden mist of rain from violet clouds
for minds in avid search of signs,
although my drive away is metaphor,
consigning present loss to mellow past,
advancing by retreat.
at 3 a.m. the world's asleep
beneath a sky
that's blushed by streetlight's amber stars
and cleansed by autumn chill,
and you are everywhere
to take your final leave,
the brief ubiquity
that's granted
when you kiss the cheek of time,
released at last from stertorous noise
and all Ward 3's disturbances.
i'm now the only person in the world,
and as the car glides noiselessly
on empty roads,
our dialogue's pure:
no need for secrets any more
or all the checks of guardedness;
we're both at peace
and will not rage
against the dying of the light.

Laurie Brady

Previously published in *Rummy*, Ginninderra Press, 2013

Boxed-up Corners

She was a child,
free as May day mist,
latchkeyed, unfettered by rules
unbounded by boundaries
no good everyone said
mother dead long ago overdosed
father at home but drunk in stupor
the bottle almost always empty

no one there to wipe
the bruised knees of
her unchildhood
a schoolday bully's dream
no good everyone said
she churned life's lessons to bad choices
vulnerability hardened overtime
to self-sufficiency
adolescence smoked to lift the pain
injected to deaden it
no good everyone said

poverty stains through the soles
of her worn-out shoes
walking miles without anyone
to follow in their footsteps
no good everyone said
at times she agrees
retreats
to where the crazy things reside
in the boxed-up corners of her mind

Myra King

Untamed

In swift summers, we never stop scampering,
falling from breakneck horses as snowdrifts
blacken and fade. We sprint and kick
in long grass, try tennis on wayward
bounces of makeshift potato-field courts,
fall in fading light, scar in ditches.
We climb sloping metal roofs warmed by
Mother's baking and a book, survey
all the bee-buzzed world, race to the
roiling river, swim among snags, catch
weeping willows laden with leaves, fool
the flood, bash tender flesh on dumb rocks,
shiver our way out, scale harsh bark and bask
in overhanging forks chiding the flow below.

In winter, scalded by polar winds, snow bites
our fire-breathing nostrils, washing hangs
stiff like frozen slabs of meat. We skate
above frigid fish on thin and thick fluvial
ice, dig snowdrifts from our door along long
tracks entrenched above our heads, zoom
through narrow gates on homemade sleds
an inch to spare each side, clump back on
unfelt feet, thaw and learn haphazardly
beside the monumental cast-iron stove that
cooks and heals and heats, its flues stretching
upstairs to our dreaming places, our nightmares:
children of nomads, camping this year in Quebec,
we forget our next move in the zest of now.

Ann Simic

Advice to Girl on Leaving Home

…and don't forget to pack your Wild.

Huh? says the girl.

Life will toss you
Responsibilities and demands;
Partners, children, debt,
Jobs and rent.
You'll catch them all, I expect.

But when the man's world tries to push you one way,
Your Wild will give you the power to push back.

If Little Red Riding Hood had taken her Wild with her,
She might not have needed the woodcutter to rescue her.

If Cinderella had used her Wild,
She would've ditched those wicked stepsisters
and never had to wait for some prince.

Where was Snow White's Wild
when she needed to stand up to her stepmother?

So,
Take your Wild with you when you go…
and never be scared to use it.

Linda Albertson

Wild Janus

'Twelve hugs a day'
is what my friend prescribed –
to hear her say it
drove me wild.

> I knew a man –
> a doctor man –
> who gave out hugs
> as his prescription;
> even now I feel the chill.

One close embrace
now and then
is what we need
(not an unbridled dozen)
with the warmth that counts,
the love heartfelt, an osmosis,
feeding every vein:
the receiver
wild with joy.

Betty McKenzie-Tubb

Red

The cheapest renters within walking distance of the uni,
'Moher' and 'Shandon',
two red-brick terraces built just like the pub next door,
Mulcahy's, a good walk from Victoria Docks,
solid working-class Edwardian.

From upstairs, between the wool store and the wheat silos,
the rumble of the shunting yards early in the morning.

We moved in with our one-year-old and a scholarship.

From her high chair,
the little one patted the window pane as cars unloaded
sides of lamb, cases of scotch,
small electrical appliances –
every tenth pallet dropped as a matter of course.

I thought I should meet the neighbours to show goodwill.

'Don't worry, mate,' said a huge fellow called Red,
'You've got nothin',
We've been through your place already.
But watch yourself – gets a bit wild of a Thursday night.'

We got used to the ten-thirty ritual of murderous voices
swearing everlasting friendship,
the crash of glass on the bricks of the wool store opposite,
and the low growl of Red's voice, unmistakable:

'Hey, quit it youse blokes, there's a baby asleep upstairs!'

Christopher Nailer

Five Hours Late

Pupils dark and piercing
        bloodshot globes
wild twins in your scarlet face
        drunken brain spinning
                my words.

Walls shrink back
        as your body towers
to its full height
        slow, harsh, intake of breath
through clenched teeth
        and lips thinned ready
to spit caustic words
        with stale alcohol fume.

A fly cowers on far side
        of lampshade
alert for violence
        and chaotic voices.

Jean McArthur

Freedom Fighter

He wore the badges on his chest.
By ten, his first was raised,
Back in the glory days.
And he marched beside his comrades
And he learnt to use a rifle
And he stormed the barricades.
Shining path, fighting songs, people's war,
Red beret, raise the flag.
Braveheart.

His path was with the people.
Oppressed by foreign rule,
They saw violence as the way.
Justice for the citizens,
Take back what is ours.
We will triumph.
One day.
Single-minded, dedicated to the cause.
Revolutionary ideology.
Leader.

He fed them with his energy
His comrades killed by shells –
All for some greater good.
The rebel stronghold held
While he resisted in the mountains
And the streets dissolved in blood.
Activist, socialist, idealist.
Soul on fire. Never tire. Martyr.
His truth is marching on.

Lisa Milner

Previously published in *The Fourth Saturday: Twentieth Anniversary Anthology*, Nambucca Valley Writers Group

Ride the Wind

If I could ride the wild wind
and catch the end of his coat,
would he bring me,
golden straw tousled hair,
eyes blue bright a starry night,
cheeks flushed pink as berries bright,
to you.

Jennifer Sinclair

Previously published in *Heavenly Seduction and other poems*,
Ginninderra Press, 2018

Captured

When the wildness comes it sets her free
a will-o'-the-wisp impossible to contain
unbridled, unfettered with a quick witted brain
likely to turn a good man insane.
When the wildness comes do not let her be
unruly, rowdy, disorderly and lawless
her madcapped behaviour must be removed
her asinine ramblings be improved
as she becomes an embarrassment in public places
this stormy behaviour is sure to disgrace us.
When the wildness comes can't you see
an unbridled, chaotic slant to her that,
while amusing in small quantities,
cannot fit. She must be cultivated, refined,
educated, unwanted impurities removed
so elegance can shine. Impeccable to her fingertips
no boorish coarseness issuing from pretty lips.
Only then will she find a man
who will help her take her stand and consummate her natural place.
As a wild woman she is a disgrace to family, gender, the proper order of life.
The wild woman must be captured and shaped into wife.

When the wildness comes it lurks in her eyes
a flint of passion there then gone
for the wildness has left her it no longer belongs
in this tame world structured to insure
the wildness will not set her free as before.

Janette Dadd

Jungle Predators

You encroach upon my territory
Eyes flashing   claws ready to strike
Adrenalin rushes   I hiss
My fur bristles   I bare my teeth
We stand in dense scrub
Of our personality clash
Crouching   poised
Wondering who will
Be the first to
Go for the jugular.

Kathy Abrahams

Vegemite

For Sasha Ruby at eight months

You terrify – and delight – me
the way you gnash with your teeth
which you don't actually have yet
that piece of crust
with the merest smear of Vegemite,
your first taste of it.

After all the bland stuff you're fed
it smacks of the ferocious way
you will one day, in the future
attack Life.

We dread, but long for too,
the day you'll take off,
your parents in pursuit.

Ros Schulz

Fence Down

Having been out there for hours, the fence down again,
he came slowly back in from the garden, the wind
buffeting him, his sparse hair taking flight; then the slam
of the door, the flap of coat and the uneasy settle
to the hushed atonement of the kitchen. 'I'll have to go back out.
I'm too stiff for now.' A ghost, haunting me with his last
authority, his grey, watery gaze, distant still, fathoming
what's left to it; a scoured crow foraging amongst pickings.

'Don't marry that boy, he's too wild,' said my mother's
mother. 'Like being out in a rough wind.' How he would
flirt with them all in the air-raid shelter, dare the bombers
defy him; lean cockily smoking up against the hay bales
tempting the lit end to the stalks; steal out on a cold night
to swap around all the neighbours' underwear
hung up on their lines for the next day; brick up
their front doors; risk, make game of; like the world
gave cause to be teased out, mixed up, disturbed.
Now it was the weather slapped back at him,
blowing down fences, pressing the world's own
irregularity through things; all got too serious to be
played up to now, toyed with. I could feel the trouble
that had grown into his heart, the worn-down tautness
of his face, the long thinking of things being never how
they should be; difficult even to keep equal with what is
when what is, is always hurrying at you too. Like it came
blustering up the path then, stiffening the slack
of the empty clothes lines, as I watched him again holding
ground at the top of the garden with the few last birds,
the broken laps of fencing askew as life, and as hard to put back.

Philip Radmall

Y/our Dark

Our days should have been
startling as mountain pepper
in an alpine snow bloom;
our night walks redolent
of lemon mint breezes
with meteorites sparking;
but that incessant wind
provoked your clouds,
inciting mare's tail wisps
to stampedes of thunder.
Was your spirit fused in some dark spiral,
the coda of a distracted love
that flagellated towards your quickening?
Are so charged with wild voltage
that you cannot slow
to share a blossom shower
in a summering spring,
or the ferment of apples
on autumn rain leaves?

Anne Morgan

Carnal Spirits

Opening over the valleys of Firenze,
miraculous flooding light of every day,
these ornate doors slide on ancient tracks,
are heavy with the histories of a thousand lovers.
They part, surely, on paradise,
our limbs entangled, blessed.
Or so we imagined,
fearing otherwise, eyes turning
towards the far fields –
the guilty sighing, the burning 'if only' –
of eternity.
Should we now join that tumultuous chorus of regret –
Cressida and Troilus, Francesca and Paolo,
Gustave and Tadzio, Vronsky and Anna –
falling down without hope
beside the multitudes who loved unwisely,
groaning in the darkening air?
But you have cleaved to me, and I to you,
down all these long, hungry years
in which we loved and grieved,
loved and grieved.
Is it virtue or stubbornness or greed
that makes us hold on?
Your hand reaches out
to close the doors, to undress all fears,
your wild amorousness my only key.
Love, that *exempts no one beloved
from loving*, seizes us
with a joy reborn, so strong
it cannot desert us, we carnal spirits.

Lyn McCredden

...and a new road

Where the wavewall rises to the sky
and scrapes the dark with a jarring thunderous threat,
the ambered moment sets in sudden, silent pause:
a moment twin-dimensioned, held within the confines of a past
inhabited by a shifting turbulence of lives
and an empty future burdened by the debt
of hope. So, the anaesthetic soundless moment roars
unheard by those whose every moment is their last.

Behind the wave, a fluid state of persecution:
the night-time raids that torture follows –
electro-probes, cigarette burns, the casual raping –
visited indiscriminate on men and women, young and old.
Relief is found only in soundproofed, screaming execution
that the blind-eyed Western world is prepared to swallow
as factional exaggeration (even though there's no escaping
the ever-growing missing lists that continually unfold).

Ahead, survival – in a world defined by mute indifference
like the invisibility of shadow under cloud.
Maybe civilisation will be reclaimed in a café coffee cup
or on a bus ride along dull and ordinary roads…

Or maybe, when the Jericho wave annihilates all chance
of wild-imagined choices, when the boat is ploughed
beneath the water, overturned and bottomed-up,
the endgame is Nauru. And all life, at last, implodes.

Janey Mac

Where else we can find history besides in the words of the victors

The hills still talk
They pour the good stuff forward
The way they once spewed molten lava

The stats talk
Subaltern distress
Despite no proven genetic disposition

The descendants of the
Half-castes
Quarter-castes
Octaroons
They got good stories
You know what kind that mob

And out on the lands
The oldest living culture
Still hunting
Still dancing
On earth

Linda Wells

Wild Bereavement

you can't do that…

…leave me here in the emptiness
even a cat knows to climb the walls
rub up against the furniture

nothing seems different
but nothing is the same
nothing has moved

but there's more space
no one lights
the lamp by your chair

there's no other set of footsteps
on the staircase
no tea in your cup

something's not starting at its usual time
something doesn't happen as it should
someone was always, always here

then suddenly disappeared
stayed disappeared
refuses to be found

if you can do that
so can I
just help me disappear

to you

Elizabeth Goodsir

Maniots

Far from Greece's mainland, in the southern Peloponnese,
The Mani – a rugged region of rocky mountains –
Stretches a tentacle into the Mediterranean.

Harsh landscape breeds tough characters,
Rebellious, self-sufficient, often insular,
Villagers may have never left their birthplace
And know little of Greece beyond their home.
Isolated on their wild peninsula,
Maniots have a distinctive dialect,
As if to stress their separateness.

Many live a simple life,
Harvesting olives, tending goats,
Coaxing crops from stony soil.
At times of feuds and vendettas,
Maniots built homes like fortresses –
Stark stone towers high on the hills,
Strongholds for protection
And to watch for alien invaders.

Yet travellers need not fear
These independent inhabitants.
There is always a welcome
For discerning travellers
Who value the traditional ways
Of this unfrequented outpost.

Jill Nevile

Tamed?

She was told…
Don't put that in your mouth, it's not clean!
She did not explore this way again.

She was told…
Don't wander, bad people will take you away.
She stayed close to home.

She was told…
You don't need boys, have a career.
She studied hard and had no boyfriends.

She was told…
Don't have sex before marriage, you'll get pregnant.
She did, she was on the pill, and she was punished.

She was told…
Get married, have kids and stay at home.
She did but kept working.

She was told…
Don't have THAT operation, your marriage will fail.
She left her husband, but not for that reason.

She was no longer told…
She was judged.
Did she care, yes. Did she mind, yes.
But now, she was free to be her.

Annette Jolly

In the Wilds of My Mind

Forests reach into the sky
where the sombre clouds skulk by
and stark shadows multiply
in the wilds of my mind.

I hear savage creatures roar
and those clouds begin to pour.
Have I courage to explore
the vast wilds of my mind?

Now the creeks are overflowing
while the shadows keep on growing.
I have no clear way of knowing
all that's wild in my mind.

While I wish my mind would clear
and be far less dark and drear,
I find I still hold dear
the great wilds of my mind.

Kristin Martin

Beach Walk, Binalong Bay

A woman with a cut bruised face,
Perhaps from a 'domestic', has
Gone limping for a swim and left
A man to hold her clothes and wait,

To kick in a confusion of
Embarrassment, atonement, rage
The sand while scowling sideways from
Beneath a lowered brow at me,

Endangered chance witness to his
Emotionally explosive mix.
Afraid to pass I pause and gaze
Fixedly out to sea, pretend

I'm unaware he's struggling to
Keep the lid on. But tension builds
And he lifts it, moves towards me,
Just having hurled his armful at

Her coming from the briefest dip,
Brushes provocatively close,
And still not getting me to look
Storms off snarling 'fuckin' coward!'

Graeme Hetherington

DNA

What's in a name? Heritage is such
a shifting concept, rooted in different soils
and cities, inimitable balance of hybrid genes
      growing and spreading like weeds.
One of my cousins wasn't stuck on family,
said, 'thank god we can choose our friends.'

But, needing to know
before the rising darkness, where I came from,
I spat into a test tube and sent the sample off
      to some distant laboratory for analysis,
like trusting your heart to be weighed
at the judgement day (and not found wanting).
The answer came back: only 56% British (good),
plenty of Scandinavian input, French, German
      a smattering of Italian, Greek and Irish
and best of all, answer to a poet's prayer,
6% Iberian Peninsula, patterned in the DNA
      of distant cousins. Did Spanish smugglers
invade British shores, or sneak into the homes
of wives and daughters (descendants or forebears
of the convict Bragges)?

Like Tennyson's lotus-eaters, or Arnold's
grave Tyrian trader, who sailed to where
shy traffickers, the dark Iberians come,
      and on the beach undid his corded bales
each generation has its scholar-gypsies
its changeling children.

                        Margaret Bradstock

For My Son

Wild days they were,
wild winds blew, fanning the
flames of the fires burning on
the hills above Ti-Tree Gully.
The birth had been quick.
Was the wild day a portent?

He worked in parched plains
with the lone cries of crows
that seemed to beg for rain,
rain that never came and where
the only refreshing sight
was the sluggish movement of
the wide river and reflected gum trees.

A wild man he was, my son,
a man of deep passions,
his only escape from his loneliness
the words he placed so carefully
on the page. Here grief and deep pain
gathered together huddling against
the bleak days and nights.

Wild words he wrote
of a distant land and a lover
too far away for any comfort.
Flowering hedgerows, foreign skies,
words from a land of poets.

Dorothy Hansen

It's an Emergency

an ambulance lights flashing siren squealing
makes a pit stop at the Chardon's Bottle-O
Drive-Through and a man calls out through the
wound down window for immediate assistance
he says they're low on anaesthetic for a
patient and he needs two bottles of vodka

for the guy in the back cos he's lost a lot
of blood and he is in incredible pain so can
he get a six-pack of Coors light and a litre of
tequila and a lime as they may not make it
to the hospital in time and also maybe some
salt and vinegar crisps and a packet of peanuts

and some Marlboro man is this a tough job the
driver says lighting up a smoke and paying through
the wound down window with some fifties
the ambulance screams off into oncoming
traffic and the naked medic tied up and
gagged in the back hopes the madman with

the ruptured liver who bound and muzzled him
and took his wallet is going to do the
sensible thing and drive the stolen ambulance
back to the hospital as soon as possible
as the crazy bastard doesn't have long to live

Dominic Kirwan

Urban dis-ease

It's difficult
for many children nowadays
surrounded by cement, asphalt and bricks
phones, iPads, laptops
air conditioning.

I pity them
their lives contained by ease
far from muddy steams, twisted trees
waiting to be climbed.

I wish them an opportunity
to venture into the wild and see
down steep slopes, between tall trees
small orchids unfurl and rise
many-coloured butterflies.

…to taste refreshing eucalyptus leaves
sweet gum from golden wattle trees
It seems they believe
the world out there is dangerous
a dirty, unhygienic mess
a frightening wilderness.

It's not too late!
Grandparents, grasp opportunities
build dams, campfires, tepees…
break civilisation's veneer
let the children breath deep
run free in the wild…

Rosemary Winderlich

Night Dreams

Wild my night dreams
since you vanished
shadowless into the sun-filled day.

Deep when I reach through
the velvet darkness of your shade
hovering above me
warm and moist like mist over a lake.

Tears deny sleep and
I pace the corners of our house
cobwebbed with memories that
cling and circle me in the noose of
love's lethal knot.

Smiles from the mantelpiece
taunt and meander
the chambers of my artful heart.

Tormenting trickster
you are virga to me now
rain that evaporates before
it touches the ground

Breeze that stirs my hair
ever-present but invisible
except when you visit unbeckoned
and I am wrapped in you
wild in my night dreams.

Mary Pomfret

A Wilderness

A wilderness
Overwhelms my soul
Unleashing its tremors
And irregularities,
Forming awareness
Of soft frailties
And wonderful complexities;
The heights and summits
Of pulsating ecstasies.

I breathe through
The tides of anguish
And plummeting depths.
The soft meanderings
Induce peaceful rest
That soothe and relieve
My weary soul.

I climb and soar
Each tempestuous peak,
Returning within
To where my heart beats.

Melanie Duncan

My firstborn

My heart is singing a song to the world, and the feeling's simply wild,
It's a song of hope and happiness, it's a song for my firstborn child.

I never guessed in a million years, just what the feeling would be,
To hold you close in my arms each day, another branch on our family tree.

I tried to imagine what it would be like, to meet you for the very first time,
You're not like anyone I've ever met – you, my child, are mine.

You see no matter how hard I tried to guess, how our time together would start,
I never imagined the love I'd feel and the pride that fills my heart.

I never knew how something so small, so delicate and new,
Could change the way I see the world and change my priorities, too.

Your skin, your eyes, your little nose, the sound you make when you cry,
You make us want to be the best we can – of that, be sure, we'll try.

And since you arrived in the world last week, it's never seemed so bright,
Life has never seemed so grand, so glorious and light.

It's a feeling that I've never known, so many emotions rolled into one,
It's a feeling that makes me reach for the stars, knowing you, my boy, are my son.

It's a feeling that has me jumping for joy, that I'm your dad, and you're my child,
I'm singing, I'm dancing, I'm over the moon – the feeling is simply wild!

Sam Duncan

'To seek solitude like a wild animal.
   That is my only ambition.'

Dalai Lama

Silver brumby

Hunted for the moon in his coat
he looks downriver
from tumbled rocks

like some sure-footed god

Wild and gleaming
he listens to what the wind
tells him

reads the snowgrass and skies
makes a deal
with the coming storm

that he will lead its lightning
when they track closer
make them believe

they chase nothing but a ghost

J V Birch

The Tyger

Tyger Tyger, striped and lean,
Marsupial thylacine,
What immortal mind might think
To make one such as you extinct?

Blame the bounties, blame the dogs,
Blame the sawn and rolling logs,
Blame disease, the human slur,
No one really knows for sure.

Some say the last one of its kin,
Went by the name of Benjamin.
No proof or records of that tale:
The photographs suggest female.

In what bush, in what brush,
In what dry eucalyptus,
Nocturnal hunter, quiet and shy,
Hid thy graceful symmetry?

Tyger Tyger, striped and lean,
Marsupial thylacine,
Did we glimpse thee on that track?
Perhaps a clone will bring you back

Joe Dolce

Previously published in *The Australian Poetry Journal*, Volume 5, Issue 2, November 2015

Warrigal

Dingo-trickster – Aboriginal Dreamtime

An omen of crows swoops
feathered shields dip   dissolve boundaries
Sun Mother walks the world into being
Warrigal greets her in stripes
of shadow and light, a twist of tail
flows down the sacred road
world survivor on the edges of vision
changes skin gathers faces
a mystery in clever phrases.

White teeth foam in the wake of his laugh
his song carves the bones of past magic
where Day peels its skin of shadows
and Night wraps truth in purple
pulling the world
into his dance.

Wind pauses
watches sun fold itself into shadows
torching cloud underbellies
Dingo presses paws   twists leaves
burying sound. An apparition
trading in confusion
eyes flicker inhabiting air
in the moment of his vanishing.

Gail Willems

'River Horse'

From ancient Greek – hippo (horse) potamus (river)

A weighty fellow, he wades and wallows
in the Zambezi, as pink fingers of light
play on river ripples.
The barrel shape sinks, submerges,
and tree-stump legs bounce
and slosh, a cement mixer
of murky mud.

Then in the glaring African sun,
his ears and nostrils skim the surface,
and periscope eyes dart deftly
to detect danger.
Bearing lethal tusks, he grunts,
snorts and bellows
like a honking horn to repel prey.

At dusk, he emerges, yawns,
a gaping chasm.
Content, he grazes on grasses
along banks, surveys the scene,
and later, with the hint of a smile,
he waddles back
into the wild waters of home.

Shelda Rathmann

Wolf

Wolf hunting in a pack,
Thriller,
       Invader, hunter-killer,
                   slipping into
                           Peaceful pastures
             With
                 Your
                     Dark
                           Leanness,
Like a sliver of night,
       Dark wedge in the sunlight,
While your raw, doleful keening interrupts the choirs of birds,
Fallen silent, in fear, songs strangled.
               WOLF

You are like the shadows in dark, suburban places.

Adriana Wood

Previously published in *Sleeping On Trains*, Ginninderra Press, 2012

All on a summer's day

Twycross Zoo, Warwickshire, UK

Avalanches of snow leopards
tumble over one another
on shelves and tabletops
of souvenir shops and cafés
by the exit.
'Try before you buy' the sign says
and they had –
those children and newly coupled sweethearts
having passed by *the real thing* already
sun-drenched and on display
within the zoo.

Secreted there
beneath the small overhang
of a rocky mound
in a hopeless pool of shade
the snow leopard shimmers and melts
beyond the chilled glass wall of
the air-conditioned café
where lovers and kids alike
clutch cold drinks and hot chips –
wild about their cool new furry friends.

Jane O'Sullivan

Stamped with the Caption

My home is under a railway bridge;
I shuffle about in the dust.
Now and then visitors offer bananas
in hesitant finger-filled fear.
Occasionally they might pay for a ride
then all the iPhones will click.
Souvenirs are available, made from fake leather
or plastic, transported from factories in Dacca.

Each evening I hobble along with my keeper
down to the river to wash,
disco lights on tourist boats winking.
People on deck point and wave.
Activists want me returned to the wild
(plantations have taken its place).
Supporters assembling with slogans on placards
are handcuffed and hurled into cells for their trouble.

Deep in my memory an image persists
where there's nothing but foliage and trees.
Shadows of animals pass in the distance;
I trumpet, but none of them hears.
Wrap me in all the green places you've seen
as years of my life lumber on.
Go home in that tee shirt. The one with my picture,
stamped with the caption I LOVE…

Hazel Hall

Under the panda cam

At the zoo beside the bamboo-fringed pool
the pandas are peeping through
their window of opportunity.

They assess each other's powers of attraction,
share common interests, compare tastes
in roots and shoots

before making physical contact: bumping, patting,
rolling, stroking; paws palpating, tongues tasting,
playing chequerboard games of Pass and Jump.

They are the yin and yang of youthful exuberance;
the black and white barber's pole twist
of panda play.

But now the patterns unravel. Bodies disconnect,
pink mouths yawn: no opportunities taken
and the window closing.

Judy Dally

Mother says

'It could almost be,'
says she to me,
daily.
'Ignore the bus and the humans therein.
Close your ears, no engine din.
Hold your breath, rid diesel from your lungs.
And we could be…
but not quite…
Slink low in this shrubbery
under the leaves so Aussie gummery.
We're not in Africa, out on the veldt –
the elephant long, long gone.
But here in the tall dry grass
watch the giraffes beyond…
the fence, double electric.
Try just a little, my dear.
Accept that you, a cheetah rare,
are treasured enough to be
imprisoned here in this strange place.
See the emu under the gum.
He has an ostrich-like run.
There are meerkats down below
and at night we hear the lone hyena howl.
Enjoy your camouflage,
trick tourists with your ruse.
We have overhead sky so blue,
it is almost a wondrous African hue.
Don't fret my pet, my curly bub.
Do let's pretend we're in the wild.
Once again.'

Alice Shore

On the Wolf Trail

I am a wolf –
always preferring to observe.

I keep swift feet,
avoiding body contact in close.

Loose skin
hanging around my neck

never permits
sink-searching fangs.

Fur between pads
is all that can be traced before pouncing,

assertive only
to restore nature's equilibrium.

I feel stronger roaming alone
than in a pack.

As my kind
find it difficult to bark,

peripheral and night vision
detect dogs.

They search for a master –

I am always hunting for a place.

Martin Jon Porter

Thylacinus cynocephalus

Declared extinct in 1986

Tassie Tiger, you still burn bright in fever dreams
emerging from the deceitful shadows of our past.
From misty rainforest, tangled scrub, desperate hope.

Poor Tiger! You burned too bright for the graziers to bear.
Blamed for sheep torn by feral dogs, like the human natives,
you were shot, hanged, caged. Your light dimmed, snuffed

Out in a Hobart jail in nineteen thirty-six. Still our faith
in Immortal Thylacine lingers, fanned by ardent believers.
Tasmanians cannot conceive of our island without a living

Thylacine. Sketches of a shy tiger peering through leaves
don't satisfy. We must see (and touch?) a living one. Now
DNA's been drawn from the last (stillborn) pup, the dream's

Morphed: cloned tigers. It won't do. The thylacine is Tassie's
Lasseter's Reef. Fanatical believers will continue searching
As our ghostly thylacine slips silently through the shadows.

Sue Cartledge

Bomber's Moon

Unfamiliar with the terminologies of war,
these dogs still know
this is the night.
With a sharp yelp to spur on a loiterer,
they lope with ease over the frosted hills.
Their target a huddle of silly goats
packed into the paddock's corner,
shivering in moonwash.

Aroused in their shed, two dogs
quiver to the memory of an ancient code.
With hoarse and hectic barking,
they lunge at the door that keeps them safe,
yearn for that dark gully.
Ignorant, we force them still.

A rush on the ridge line.
There is blood and open-wounded horror.

Morning. Muzzles twitching at scents beyond us,
our dogs race to pee the fence posts,
before wolfing down their breakfast pellets.

Margaret Collett

David Attenborough: The Life of Mammals

Last night
On the television
Green treetops and
A band of monkeys
Playing.

Shrieks of alarm
Chimpanzee hunters

Flying shapes now
Light fractured through leaves:
One falls
Is snatched up
Grimace of teeth
And dark eager
Hands.

Half-hidden by foliage
Clutching her baby
Another waits
Gibbering.

Left; right:
Up; down:
The eyes in her small face
Distressingly human
Any one of us,
Powerless,
Caught in a war zone.

Zenda Vecchio

Natural Habitats

Hush! Be still, turn eyes up to the trees
watch the koala there, munching
on his eucalyptus leaves peacefully
busy with his day-long lunching
in the wild

Watch for kangaroo and wallaby
when travelling though the outback
go quietly when you wish to see
the animals in their natural habitat
in the wild

Respect the land, understand this place
where creatures live their special lives
unaware of creed or race, of humans
who come with guns or knives
into the wild

In the desert, mountains, forests, plains
are creatures, some you'll never see
and they'll never know that anyone came
if you go with care, respectfully
into the wild

So be vigilant, remain always aware
that these are creatures who are free,
they may not like your presence there
so be in awe but let them be
in the wild.

Edna Taylor

Because, like the weather

Because, like the weather, it colours this place
you do not notice. Maybe, you'll sense
in the way something is put, something avoided –
neatly, often a smile – that though friendly enough,
no matter how long you have been among them
you can't be trusted to understand. How could you?

      So, I tell this as an anecdote.
They'd been seeing it for some time,
even caught sight of it padding by the back door,
its stink down by the chook pens,
but now it's here, in a cage they'd set
with one of the lambs it has killed.

There is panic in the froth of saliva.
Eyes engorged with brilliance.
      Their dogs, the fox.
They bay and snap at the cage.
It is sweat-matted and concentrates its stare
on its newest threat, swivels and snarls,
and tears at air and is lost in the mash of its fate.
      One by one
a new dog is introduced
until terror extinguishes with a yelp.
The cage, silent as the hills,
      as all witness is.
'The best way to blood pups,' he says.
Trusting me with that much.

Russell Erwin

meerkat at a summer *milonga*

meerkat at a summer *milonga*
watches the sleek calligraphy of *milongueras*
his bright eye a wide open stare
tango music electrifies the air
he preens his smooth physique, dreams
he is a *milonguero* but
clearly, he doesn't know
his *ochos* from his elbow.

alert to every sound
he twirls, he swirls around
attempts some rhythmic steps
oh me, oh me, meerkat
his artful tail flicks fall flat
lost in tango, forgets he is a mere *kat*.

Avril Bradley

milongueras: female tango dancers
milonguero: male tango dancer
ochos: complicated tango steps

Winner of the Wild Tango Poetry competition, 2016; previously published in *Tango Australis*, June 2016

On the Daintree River

At 4 p.m. Ray greets us smiling, tattooed from neck to ankles.
It turns out he knows a bit about crocodiles.

'Ray, what do crocodiles eat?'

'Mate, they eat whatever they bloody well want.
I call that one Scarface. He weighs at least five hundred kilos.
What you see above the water is only about ten per cent of him.
At 29 kilometres an hour he'll hit you like a bus with teeth.
He'll take pigs, humans and even his own hatchlings.
He can smash a fully grown cow like a tic-tac.'

No one's sure if they should laugh or shit themselves.
But Ray's a friendly guy. He tells it like it is.
It comes from years of cruising this river.
He spots a yearling in mud. It's invisible to us.

'I've been bitten by one that size a few times.
It feels like your finger's been hit with a hammer.
Mate, when they made the first saltwater crocodile
They got it right. No need for upgrades.'

Ray says they're the psychopaths of the animal kingdom. Pure instinct.
Remnants of a world before humans confused things.

'Ray, do you ever eat crocodiles?'

'Mate, I don't eat them and I try not to let them eat me.'

Mark Mahemoff

The Wildest Beast

Earth's wildest beasts, with tooth and claw,
with tusk and brawn and powerful jaw
inhabit forest, plain and sky,
oceans, rivers, and defy
attempts to tame their jungle law.

We build our empires, land laid raw.
Despite the fear, we won't withdraw
but wishing always to deny
the wildest beasts.

As earth's resources overdraw
we fail to see our fatal flaw.
The earth itself is heard to cry,
as creatures round us fail and die,
'You are the wildest beast.'

Margaret Clark

Anjing Warrior

Pejuang anjing: dog warrior

Make no mistake!
I am the Alpha!
I am the grief you fear.
I loom and the
Order is in place and
I make the order –
I put it there;
the pecking order;
a line of the meek-mutts;
and they're waiting,
waiting for the odds.

David Taylor

Previously published in *Life Scraps*, Picaro Poets, 2017

Not in the wild at all!

You call this 'in the wild'?
Your cushy beehive-shaped nest
a basket perched on a pole
with a tray of yummy fruit
parked quite near
in the Melbourne zoo.

Far from the dark forests of Madagascar
No predators licking their lips
No tractors felling your trees
No threat of extinction

Jump to it, ring-tailed lemur
Jump with your long striped tail streaming
Jump into your basket nest
Leave your haunting cries
and shut your staring eyes
Settle down for a quiet night's rest
Moonbeams gently caress
Your babies snug in your embrace.

Dream on…

Margaret Bolton

'Wilderness is more than a natural place,
more than a place for recreation.
It is a place for inspiration.'

The Wilderness Society

Camping on the edge of the Nullarbor

During the night
a soft wind rose and covered the plain
like a mourning mother searching for a lost child,
every leaf
whispering
her grief.

Russ Talbot

Previously published in *Things That Make Your Heart Beat*, Picaro Poets, 2015

Night on Blackhorse Creek

Night has climbed out of the valley,
stealing from the leopard gums
their last fuss of colour.

Through the black heart of scrub
no light warms a welcome.

The day has put to bed its darlings,
whipbirds, goannas, bard frogs –
have all retired for the night.

But under the lantana
pythons slither, ready to dine
on unsuspecting ducks.

Pademelons charge our car
in blind kamikaze assaults
as it yo-yos down the rutted track.

Suddenly   from over the hill
a shrill tantrum of air –

the Wind lifts her skirts
and twirls between treetops,
flirting with the Devil's Snare.

She summons up the ghosts
of long-dead scrub-dwellers,
their voices still crooning
ballads of plaintive regrets.

Cary Hamlyn

on empty

On a hot day the North-West Plain is so flat it isn't.
The horizon curves and stirs like a wisp of moustache.
Animals burrow that aren't meant to burrow.
Prey walk past their predators under a white flag.
The eyes of roadkill are left to boil in their sockets.
The can of beer is dry when you open it.
A cigarette is rolling another swagman.
The motor smokes nervously before you start it.
The mobile phone sweats, whimpers and croaks.
The devil is on holiday in Tasmania.
The paddock on the left is Texas.
The seat of government is the only tree.
We'll take a rest stop at the next mirage.
Is it far? It has been. Are we there yet? No.

John Carey

Wilderness was a sentence

The word *panic* once meant to feel the fear
of wilderness, imagining the god, Pan,
with his untamed tastes, appearing
from the smiling dark of forest
before you could scream.
A place of fairy tales where children wander
into forests, a place of witches & wolves,
who know no straight lines or need light
to know who they are.
Then the trees were cut and canopies collapsed
allowing light to dissolve the dark to create settlements,
which is another word *to feel at ease*,
to stay in one place, not to venture out,
to know that things will not/can not
appear suddenly at your door with the wet
smell of undergrowth in its pores or long
scrape of claw at the wooden door.
And so it was from the beginning
that the wilderness was a sentence,
a punishment for transgressors,
and the word 'wilderness' from *will* –
to be *wilful, uncontrolled* – was a place
where they were sent beyond the borders:
the exile of sinners, wild men who found frontiers
though it was only those who got lost in the forest
who learnt who they were, learnt that the wilderness
was not separate.

Roland Leach

Brachina Gorge

Wilpena Pound

a presence,
a twitch of a bell
in trees above the gully

grey bush
against harsh walls
caverns
alert with eyes
eagles high
on the edge

walking through
fold and fracture,
the scrambled dust of time,
the filtered sun
of the afternoon
seems to spell
all things alive
are settled now
and the tremor of change
distant
as a bird call,
close as the touch of a leaf.

Pam Morris

Kati Thanda-Lake Eyre

… I do think that Australians are saucer dwellers largely – John Olsen

The middle of the saucer is Lake Eyre –
where endlessness, where nothingness collide;
the essence of it, that it's there, but not there.

Dry, salt-encrusted plains for endless years
until rare spates of flooding swell the void
and spilling rivers push towards Lake Eyre.

With water comes life; news joyrides the air
while great flocks of birds glide in from all sides.
Somehow they know if it's there, or not there.

With water comes light – opalescent, rare;
the sun spreads a palette through milky divides
as Olsen returns, compelled by Lake Eyre.

He finds new abundance, remembers it bare –
each paint-wash drawn from a deep, inner guide;
each mark, to tell what was there, or not there,

like the salt bed's *sinister white veneer –*
how it rises again as waters recede.
The middle of the saucer is Lake Eyre,
the essence of it, that it's there, but not there.

Gillian Telford

Reference: *Look* magazine AGNSW March–April 2017, 'the you beaut country' exhibition

Note: italicised words are John Olsen's.

The Mountain's Song

The massive mountain towers above the lake,
Cold icy wind and cliff's sharp edge cut marrow.
The endless halt of time frozen solid.

An effigy in the brown heartless earth,
Where no soft indent of a small warm body
Can find a comfort cleft, nor sanctuary.
An endless plain, the withering vastness of it all.

My eyes lift again to the jagged mountain top,
Her deathly grip on me hidden in a mantle
Of impressionable pure white silken snow.
A singular cloud whipped disc-like at her crown.

But hear! Small gurgle of a stream not frozen over,
And silence broken by an eagle's cry.
And see! A small green bud between the rubbled stones.
There is life, and a kind of melting sadness in my soul.

Catharine Steinberg

Bush Tucker Tour

We take a well-worn track out to a stand
of desert *witjuri*, watch
the women dig deep, hack at the treasure
curled safely among the roots
They offer a native snack, a bush challenge
to visitors from the city
– a creamy morsel wriggling on a stick
soft and nutty in the mouth or
a roasted puffball, the comforting hint
of chicken held on the tongue

Grandmas with dillybag and stick
once sustained whole families
– the yield from a single tree
an easy meal to fill a hunter's belly
We smell the familiar scent of wattle
as they smoke *tnyeme* brush
sip a healing tea, bitter as any bush medicine
Children find us a hidden treat
Honeydew, a native sweet to lick
from the underside of leaves

Brenda Saunders

witjuri: witchetty grub
tnyeme: wattle bush

Previously published in *Quadrant*, September 2017

Return to the Desert

A landscape flat
unto distant hills
sand, soul,
drought-gripped shrub and stone
is unity
a track of the perentie
traced under a serpent staff

I am
under a blazing orb's
half-sky
white yellow dazzling sunrise
shadow chasing
melding all on the rack
of sublimated burning

dual serpents turning
two ways into power
dismissive
of the day's mirage
elusive
in truth and seeming.

Adrian Rogers

Excursion To Windjana Gorge

The Kimberley, Western Australia

Our Land Cruiser whips the track into red, ballooning dust
And broad-eared cattle stand in the worn patches of shade.
Overhead, black whistling kites sail through antique boabs
And termite nests tilt to the shape of melting birthday cakes.

As the dust blooms and settles,
The sun fingers the struggling plants on the ridges
And the ripples left by ancient seas on the walls.
Neat as a flower carefully pressed,
An antique fish lies, immortalised in stone.
Tree ants, tiny butchers in bright aprons, are dissecting a beetle.
Butterflies, fragile as embryonic flames, glide in unison.
Cockatoos bicker. Freshwater crocodiles doze and yawn,
Still as worn carpets in the brown water.

But, it is death that rules here, now.
On the water's edge, the corpse of a fruit bat lies,
Distorted like a torn, abandoned umbrella.
The bones of a kangaroo stick out from the sand,
Grim as ribs of a long-lost wreck

And, high above the cave of Jandamarra,
The wind whispers of past dispossession, murder and revenge.

William Cotter

The Diamantina

in the tortured desert where night parrots flew
from the claws of feral cats
to be barbed on fences and bilbies fled,
their burrows trampled flat,
hoteliers salved cattlemen
their glasses and hopes raised high
to the wealth and the rain and the barmaid…
that never came by;

so the termites
salvaged what they could
leaving monuments of iron
the glint of smashed glass
the pastoral shards
the mile-wide stock route lines

Jack Oats

Mawson's Hut

Douglas Mawson's Australian Antarctic Expedition, 1913

Mawson's men watched sadly
as the *Aurora* vanished beyond the bergs
Captain Davis fearing the vice-like freeze.

As he sailed through the gaps
another wild blizzard blasted the hut
mounding the snow up to the eaves.

Slowly, dark howling days were ticked
on the calendar of their second winter
so far south, yearning for home fires.

Their longing for home
poured forth in unposted letters
Mawson's to his beloved Paquita.

What a day it was when they saw
springtime's first seal
flopping onto the icy shore.

The calendar counted August days
until, magically, the *Aurora*'s mast waved
like a beacon above the bergs.

Their hearts swelled.
Douglas imagined Paquita's embrace –
they were going home.

Geoff Graetz

Desert Sand

Infinite purity,
proud and timeless,
forbidding, forsaken, magnificent.
Tidal flow defying change.

Promiscuous, masculine sand,
penetrating everything.

Soft, feminine sand,
swallows the intruder's feet,
assimilates the foreign,
swelling and ebbing like the tide
across time's spectrum,
washing away all trace of man.

Ian Coulls

Previously published in *Words*, Picaro Poets, 2017

Cradle Mountain

The landscape's skin is moist with mist and rain.
Spring has ill-defined her alpine face.
The mountain carves an image in my brain.

The sunshine seems determined to abstain.
The air is chill and sharp in its embrace.
The landscape's skin is moist with mist and rain.

The last snows, solid on the ridge, remain
a tablecloth of icicles and lace.
The mountain carves an image in my brain.

Droplets on pandanus form a chain
receding now to rest in snugger space.
The landscape's skin is moist with mist and rain.

Waterfalls slap rock with whip and strain.
Clouds tumble at an unrelenting pace.
The mountain carves an image in my brain.

Small birds whistle big in stark refrain.
Blue wrens flit, their jennies giving chase.
The landscape's skin is moist with mist and rain.
The mountain carves an image in my brain.

Fran Graham

Maralinga: Dead Country

Nothing down there
Not even a few wild Aborigines
No, nothing down there.
But there were.

Beautiful, muscular, skilful, sage
Grinding, carrying *kulati piti*
Crafting a spear with a head and a barb
Artfully joined with spinifex resin and a kangaroo tendon.

Of course they'd heard of the round-up
No way were they going to be herded in, cleared out
So they dissolved into country.

Amongst the dust, the flies and the dogs that day
Yami Lester lost his eyes
And the great earth died.

Adrian Lane

With thanks to Tarnanthi and Black Mist Burnt Country

imagining what you can't imagine…

The sail-fish and the iguana
give the lie to the science before Galapagos.
They are the best case.
They provide the proof
that allows knowledge
over belief and ignorance,
imagination over law.
So, in the waters off Galapagos
the iguanas swim
and the fish fly.

Sandra Renew

Four-wheel Drive Initiation

The predatory purring of powerful engines
like a lions' pride of four-wheel drives:
there is nothing else here,
except the closed dilapidated kiosk.
In a ragged convoy they rumble off
tuned in to instructions via UHF radio.

Sparse scrubby bushes and spindly grass
struggle in salt-white terrain, water lies stagnant
in wheel ruts and holes in the track
under a metallic blue sky.
A sense of utter desolation,
no fixed points of reference –
only the moving vehicles,
the thrumming of engines –
my mind leaps beyond the dry dunes
to the unforgiving outback, lying in wait.

We jolt and jostle over corrugations,
crawl up a steep hill, ignorant
of dangers lurking – until we crest, take a deep breath –
plunge down, down onto the muddy tracks
of those who bravely went before.
Later, I drive aslant, driver's side wheels tilted up
on a sand dune, white knuckles gripping the wheel,
a reluctant novice; off air I mutter imprecations
against all the other dauntless drivers –
especially brash four-wheel drive instructors.

Sue Cook

En Route To Alaska

The sun wakes me at sea
Vancouver Island to my left

to my right mocha seals
bask on mottled rocks.

Sitka spruces a dark mystery
– the Rockies, a snow of alabaster.

Sky and sea are celestine and silver.
Out here in the blind of morning,

I squint through binoculars and see
a bald eagle hook himself to hemlock.

His head looks like a tennis ball thrown
high into the morning air by a careless child.

Moya Pacey

Previously published in *Island* #119 and in *The Wardrobe*, Ginninderra Press, 2009

Entering the Forest…

You absorb the pungent smells and stray cries,
the sing-song chatter of squirrels, the 'tock tock' of woodpeckers,
rustles in the brush, the hovering of dragonflies…
but feel also: what could that dark shadow be?
Lost in this green world's dance your eyes are becoming heavy.
Dimly you remember the warnings and precautions
about the largest fauna – the cartoon gestures of bells and mace.
Holding your partner's hand you are lulled
as the air vibrates with a husky cough…
somewhere water is trickling,
the clock of dusk clicking closer.

The next day you wake and the old rhythms treat you as an equal;
nothing to ask for, no memory of anxiety.
You see the telltale tracks on the ground –
but now you've reached the forest's edge once more.

In your hotel that night you see the 'trial cam' in the lobby
replaying the images from the last 12 hours of darkness.

You recognise that part of the track where it forked downhill
once more you two are lying there
as the ghosts nudge by – wolf, lynx, deer, bear, cougar, wolf,
bear, deer, elk, lynx, wolf.

Danny Gardner

'The smaller the creature, the bolder its spirit.'

Suzy Kassem

The Black Snake

By the potting shed a grassy path
leans against the light.
And drinking in the golden sun:
the shivery scales of night.
Long and sleek with sinuous will
he lays uncoiled and very still.

Watching me as I watch him;
frozen with the day.
Wondering at the scheme of things
and who has right of way.

Then he moves with liquid speed:
an urgent, thrilling grace.
Vanishing as the sunlight fills
the flickering hollow space.

I stand alone upon the path
his image cold and clear.
Which will I remember first,
the beauty or the fear?

Ian McFarlane

Previously published in *The Shapes of Light*, Ginninderra Press, 2014

From the Tree

A puzzling pile of grass and sticks
with a suspicion of moving tail feathers
appeared in the crook of a branch
across the road in a tall eucalypt
seen from our kitchen window.

Later, a currawong, wolf-black with white flashes
glides from the nearby reserve to the nest
and bends down to feed a chick
that stretches up in dark profile;
long thin neck and slim fig head.

A windstorm drops the chick onto asphalt
to crouch near the fence, pale-mouthed, bedraggled.
Still there next day, it grooms its wings.
Days later, not fully fledged, it flies
to an instant parent for a feed;
an offspring, deceptively durable.

Paul Williamson

Previously published in *Quadrant*, 2015

Sanctuary

They have returned again, these two
Now summer rain has plunged into the soil
And garden trees are dense and lush and thick,
Our bedroom luminous beneath a filtered feather canopy of poinciana light.
They nestle like one mottled branch
Hunched against each other, still as driftwood
Palms whip and snap in afternoon sea breeze
But they are safe and somnolent,
Cradled below a summer veil of leaves and crimson flowers.
They mate for life, these tawny frogmouths
Lover by lover they sleep together
In the haven of our suburban tree
Waking at night to blink gold eyes,
Then glide on majestic wings to feast on the garden spoils.
Four years ago there was but one
Who perched then in a potted dragon tree
So camouflaged we ate a courtyard lunch
Without once noticing him there,
Large as a serene soft cat, dark as a dappled shadow.
But since there have been these two cached;
Under a midnight moon I've seen them fly
Silent and swift, their wings fringing the air
And heard their low, insistent grunting call
So monotonous it seemed a distant foreboding drum.

We are not unlike those wild things
We mate, we nest, we breed, we hunt, we warn
We huddle together year after year
In our safe place, tucked in with our
Frail faith in those we choose to trust, to shield, to touch, and love.

Tracey-Anne Forbes

Grasshopper

We amble through the years as though
the universe is second skin
layers of time fall away

in sheets of seasons barely noticed.
The sun lights our way from darkness
all manner of things marvellous

fail to move us any more.
I turn to children then, watch
for grasshopper shell moments

all life extinct to us
their untamed wonder gasps fill
the driest husks of time.

Ann Nadge

tree creeper

climacteris picumnus

The fire blacked out, we hauled that rubber hose
up heavy black terrain back to the truck
then we just waited in the scrub
with grinding gears and diesel smoke and other muck
a fading distant hubbub
to find ourselves in silent bush enclosed.

And then arrived the real machinery –
exquisite clockwork dull-as-a-sparrow gem
hopping across dry leaf litter
and crunching bark and rustling stem
this unfamiliar critter
jumped straight up the side of a tree!

I mean it hopped across and left the ground
inbuilt crampons spiralling around and up the trunk
on crab-rake feet
quite oversized, the body shrunk,
so agile, fleet,
while we just stood agog, earthbound.

Rob Walker

Galahs

Their crests billowed and bluffed
in a spooning rock opera
of footloose teenage cool
and off the cuff grooming tunes,
these paramours, no has-beens,
scope out the bird life scene
from the high-rise visor
of a combustion flue.
Their mockery downs
my groundling common sense
with heraldic shock jockery
and their blazon,
parted proper in cloudy bars
and charged with a lightfast plumage
of pale gules and argent,
recalls that faraway knightly buzz
of a Don Quixote joust,
where starship floods of errantry
will douse that windmill,
to fill their hearts with unruly delight,
with Sancho Panza
clouds of catastrophe,
while their pinprick eyes,
satellites of unrepentant
moonstruck brightness,
seek even more flamencos
of splendid derring-do.

Gordon McPherson

Wildlife in the City

In bushland shades, the Torrens River ripples through the Linear Park.
Wild creatures claim their territory, live in their own wild world
as wardens of the river. Strange eyes peek at me
from tangled reed beds, entwined with gregarious grasses.
I see invasive insects, long-lived lacewings,
a wandering water rat, waddling water fowl
foraging hidden food or hiding under reedy bushes.
Look closely. See my companions
in a wild world at the bottom of my street.

Restless birds flit from tree to tree, full of noise and riot, a world of freedom.
Crowds of corellas, yellow-crested cockatoos and screeching lorikeets
visit often when the liquidambar nectar feast is on.
Whoosh! In a flash they're off – this is their playground.
Leave as swiftly as they come, savour the scene
above the branches, perched on power lines.
Ducks come calling at my home, ask for breakfast,
look closely, then take flight back
to the wild world at the bottom of my street.

A pair of magpies visit my lawn almost daily.
One plunges to earth, relentlessly diving, seeking food, and then is off.
Butterflies flutter around my flower beds, never still.
At night, possums play on my roof, run in circles.
Pitter patter – murmuring loudly; by morning they are gone.
Inside my home, invisible in the murky green water of its tank,
is a reptile, a turtle flapping his flippers, seeking attention.
I wonder why we go bush. Look closely – right here, right now.
You'll find my wild world in my home, near my home
and at the bottom of my street.

Airlie Jane Kirkham

Every Frog Has His Day

It was a day so still,
even the she-oaks were voiceless.
But not the marsh frogs:
two days on from heavy rain,
storm drains still swollen,
they made the best of it,
the soft hammer blows
      of their mating calls
forging links between them.
Knowing the instinctive drive
behind froggy conversations
one might imagine
      some kind of rough translation…

How about it, babe?
In your dreams, porky!
Hey gorgeous, want to hang out?
Mum says I'm not to leave the drain
till she comes home.
Then how about you over there? Yes, you!
Sorry; I'm saving myself
for that cute one in the next puddle!
But if he hasn't hit on me by tomorrow,
      I'm yours.

Robert M. Steley

Avian

I could cry out against Nature's indifference
or admire her course, her dimension, her innovation.
She is the quick-fire bird and the regal pelican,
bodies of poetry, lyric and alate.

But what of us, her incomplete creation?
I am torn by our convolution, our inconclusion.
Was our auspice the boorish flight of noisy miners
and not the murmuring of budgerigars?

I could cry out against my disappointments,
their gravity – send them adrift, silent, spiralling,
one behind the other – and turn my bird-seeing
eye toward a closer choreography, the lightning

flashes of red-green flight, the charge of nectar
campaigns. I live where song began, in the longest
piece of music, sung by an endless line of birds
rising and falling, rising and falling.

Maggie Slattery

Commissioned by the Where Song Began project

The Dark Side of Nature

she creeps between the grasses
low and sleek
eyes blink away the darkness
with half closed lids

she stalks her prey
crouched and tense
the tip of the black tail
flicks back and forth

she hurdles the obstacles
swift and effectively
her claws accomplish the goal
dig in and kill

she lays in soft sand
content and relaxed
stomach extended
satisfied for now

Barbara Gurney

Other Species

In my long-ago garden
the old house seems much smaller   hunched down.
A corroboree of magpie sing
notes of pure joy tumble down   upon all others.
No one speaks of amazing gifts like these.

A window reflecting a thrush
we watch each other
glimpse each through the other's reflection.
He makes war upon his alter ego
silver-grey plumage defending territorial rights.
His springtime voice   bell-like and clear
like no other.

At the edge of sleep and spaces between
the call of a mopoke.
Symbol of death and wisdom
he offers the crack of mouse bones.
Never close your ears to the unspoken
where heart and mind become one.
Let your eyes see the hurt of things
the imprint of teeth and claw upon them.

At the point of a gun there are holes in the air
marking the place their souls once were.
Hanging in pairs on a barbed-wire fence
tails and talons drooping in death.
Wings spread like crucified angels adrift in the air
warnings go unheeded by the wild and the hungry.
Death becomes a nameless otherness.

Lorna Thrift Brooks

Like Thistledown

When frost rests lightly in the hollows
and gold dust sparkles on the wattles
you return. Your tinkling song drifts
like thistledown across the paddock.

Assured upon your high wire perch
you lift your head and cast joy into the breeze
as long as the day is light, promises
of love and loyalty, praise to
the bounty of spring, the sweetness of youth.

Deep in the drying speargrass tufts
you build your scrawny nest, hidden
from circling hawk and stalking crow.
If threatened you dash as decoy
into another tangle in the stubble.

Little brown song lark, bird of small consequence,
invisible as summer dew, where do you go?
We'll wait to share your song again next spring
before thistles shed their downy seeds.

Jacqui Merckenschlager

fingers

the spider-woman has a script.
you can't deviate
or she eats your family or your favourite album.
her egg sac looms over every meal.
you fight for whatever's on the table with any tooth or nail
you can find.
her smile is glacial but you know where it ends.
if she falls asleep and you go outside to play, that's it.
you're grounded in sticky silver silk
until she remembers to let you go back to work.
you sweat over every coin
and they shine as they disappear into her maw
your only reward is more saliva.
some people don't have a spider
or so you've heard. they have one of the three bears,
whichever one didn't eat goldilocks
and he gives his family honey and bees to make more honey.
it sounds amazing.
of course, the bear knows the guy upstairs. has a stay of execution
up his soft sleeve for emergency indiscretions.
the others talk about his button nose;
how cute it is, just a little cold to touch. your spider has
eight eyes to watch and you never touch her.
not even at night, when she sleeps above the bed
after tucking you in, prickly hairs lingering in the sheets.
you don't even think about touching her
because she has told you exactly what will happen
to your fingers if you try.

Ashley Capes

Mollymauk

We roll and pitch.
Our bow crashes down, rears up.
Green water flows across the deck,
flung spray drenches the wheelhouse.

A wild place is the Southern ocean.
Wind and waves race
halfway round the Earth.
Sea surface a field of chaos.

And there, image of serenity –
an albatross. Old sailor's Mollymauk,
soars and circles above the waves,
wings and body motionless. Controlled.

Mollymauk, master flyer,
in this speck of ocean
a thousand miles from any land
rides the wind above the seas,
sipping energy from the storm.

The wild seabird *knows* ocean,
as a hunter *knows* country.

David Harris

caged

up the dirt track
to the co-op
selling tools   seeds   sprays
and superphosphate
you meet the old wedge-tail

it's no one's pet   caught years ago
like a mascot it is
that old rusty cage
been under the pepper tree forever
it gets a feed
used to be out on a chain   got too vicious

from a sharp mangy face
corrugated eyes stare
claws   arthritic   clubbed
cling to the perch

when it shifts balance
lifeless feathers on one wing fan
expose a shot of dull satin green

As a child I released my father's prized birds
let them play awhile in the blue sky
she's only a child my mother said
she doesn't understand
now I'm not a child   I do understand

Colleen Keating

Animal Attraction

For Bella

We bring them home
milk-plump balls wrapped in our arms
hearts open wide.
We stamp our needs across their days
impose routines
cajole and scold to make the beast
companionable.

We delight in play
their running free within a simple world.
Inside of us
a remnant of the wild tugs on its lead
yearns to roll
beside them in the mud.

Michele Fermanis-Winward

Why we shouldn't trust birds

Because they're dinosaurs; because they laugh at us
from above; because they do so much without hands.

Because their world is ultraviolet; they can see
the magnetic field; because their outlook
is a sideways glance.

Because they form sieges, packs, cauldrons and mobs;
because their heads are in the clouds; because the phoenix isn't real.

Because their songs arise from hollow bones; their plumage
is a deliberate distraction;
because the cuckoo relies on trickery and secrecy.

Because of the white-fronted ground tyrant, the hoary puffleg,
the scale-throated hermit. And the bare-faced go-away bird,
the sombre pigeon, the satanic nightjar.

Because of the brood parasites and despotic species;
because siblicide occurs with parental approval
and cannibalism is only managed.

Christopher Palmer

Dunbogan

Northern New South Wales

Wildlife is profligate here.
A goanna strayed into the garden.
A tree snake's slick, zigzag breakdance through the feijoa –
(one lightning-quick skip
down into the grass and it's gone!)
A scouting sea eagle, glimpsed as you stand
in your bathrobe at the bedroom window.
Black cockatoos, squawking out on their dawn patrol,
then looping lazily back homeward over the mangroves at dusk.
Wattlebirds, chortling noisily all day long
in the fat-coned banksias.
Sugar gliders clambering next door's TV aerial
for their evening base jump:
scooting their wing-suited way diagonally across
to latch onto the trunk of the blueberry ash.

And, while strolling the beach this afternoon –
those six sooty-coloured dolphins
caught in the high shoulder of a wave's
tottering showcase window. Giddying to watch.
Just 10 metres out, abreast of you,
and keeping the same pace:

as if you were walking them on a leash;
or maybe they were walking you.

Paul Cliff

Scarlet Robin

There a phantom flies! – a flash
of bright red cuts my eye a gash
and empties out the hill of all
emptiness.
          My eyes fall
across its path, the briefest glance
it deigns my way with head askance.
Perched with poise, its bright eyes speak
with wit. With tied-up tongue I seek
to bridge the gulf, my tools of choice
soft squeaks and trills in its own voice.
It throws a measured squiz at me,
eyes filled with sweet simplicity.
Silence speaks.
          I look once more
upon this painted bird before
it leaves me.
     Snow-white daub above
a kali-scarlet breast, yet love
is all this colour scheme conveys.
For even if skull-perched with gaze
black and brooding, I would treasure
          this small giant of pleasure.

Maurits Zwankhuizen

Fishy Secrets

Peppercorn trees on the other side
of the backyard, past pool fence,
pool, dog run & run's far fence.
They stand either side of our pond,
where fish swish, splash & splish.

Tree's branches often droop languidly,
& remind me of gentle English lakes
where willows also droop languidly,
elegant metaphor for English upper classes all
cucumber sandwiches, ennui & tea.

Today, though, wind is hard at work,
with wildly tossed branches left & right,
up & down, twisting in ways that would
tip out any foppish lad venturing onto
such waters. But our fish are alone

at the pond, with metres of water, which
though wild at the surface, is calm & cool
down at the bottom & I'm glad our fish
will survive whatever the wind tries to do.
Fish have their own schools of thought,

unknown, unknowable, accepting food
offered, as we marvel at their splishing
on cue. But when food's gone, they go too.
What happens in the school, stays in the school –
fish keeping their secrets to themselves…

Carolyn Cordon

The Albatross

'I'll tell you a story,' the old sailor said
'Still stuck in my head
I once saw an albatross land on our deck

A ballet begins when he unfolds his wings
A six-metre span, flaps in the breeze
The silence is golden
Not even a sneeze

He hops around the deck
Showing his dance
His head takes a bow
We clap
Some cameras are clicked

He soars off the deck
Into the sky and with one last dive

He honours us all.'

Ray Clift

Tamed by Love

The bird tries to live
Wild in the urban area
Hurt, frightened
I pick her up
And give her solace
Love crosses all boundaries
Intent on saving souls
Not destroying
A unifying bold force
If you do not love
You are condemned
She got better
And I set her free,
Let her go wild
Find a mate
To be in a natural state
I looked for reason
What does love mean
Is it letting go
My bird came back
I held the door open and she flew in
Overwhelmed and humbled
I had made a friend
Whose trust confirmed
A meeting of minds
She loved me in her own way
Willing to be caged
A wild bird tamed by love.

Jean Winter

'We need the tonic of wildness… At the ·same time that we are earnest to explore and learn all things, we require that all things be mysterious and unexplorable, that land and sea be indefinitely wild, unsurveyed and unfathomed by us because unfathomable. We can never have enough of nature.'

Henry David Thoreau

Wind

Tonight the house rides on wind waves.
Branches of great gums roar.
Black breakers of air knock and clash
like divers, an onrush of dumpers.
The house coils in sea salt, tensings
and flexings of night. The wind swells
burst in foam, spray like stars.

Tonight the house rides the tempest,
the moon in torrents, a trim clipper
rigging taut in her belly of sails.
Canvas distends a drumbeat mad
rhythm to the rush of the sea. Wind-raked,
tight as wire, old tiles vibrate like masts
in a new, full-rigged clarity of air.

Tonight the house rides on wind waves,
runs her cold eastings down isobars
of rungs and ladders of falling air.
I sit alert, the very foundations
of brick, rattles of metal and pane. Wood
creaks the waves of gale, the gusts of shudder.

I listen as waves crash in the trees.
She dips her bow and punches through –
the *Cutty Sark*, the *Witch of Endor*.
Sail with the wind, run with the tide.
My house rides in a demon's whirlpool,
glides on the storm like a ship of stars.

John Egan

At Reedy Creek

A cluster of reeds is stroked by the current's whirl
as if the greenish strands are being rinsed
by the slim, cleansing hands of a skilful girl.
The creek flows clear and quick, has done since
last winter's rain, and the coiffed reeds sway.
Stripping, then tying back my tangled hair,
I dive in deep to find the bed of clay.
It's slippery smooth to hold so I work with care
in digging out the lumps of precious stuff.
Arranging the clay along the bank, I knead
it into rounded forms: when set in a rough
design, they now resemble loaves of bread;
but little loaves, all bluey-grey and white,
dense and luminous in the watery light.

Suzanne Edgar

Previously published in *Quadrant*, October 2017

Flood Proof

The flood passes me by
In a grunge run down the valley
Drenched bandit
Gathering its flotsam
        Sunlit starlit litter
The foreshore is a velodrome to lost particles
        We are told not to touch
        The sea foam
        So fizzy
        Its bubbling froth
        Is pure sewage
The tide creeps back in shock and shame
Blood line caught in a rip has had a gut full
Downdrift pitches to a silver floating tone
        Shifting the microplastics
Bloated cattle carcass
Exclaims its grief in the shallows
Twitched mast of a dinghy
        Pokes its tongue out
Of splintered waters   Split hank
Of fisherman's rope lies rotting with fish heads,
        Frayed nerves exposed
A hole gapes in the bridge's flank
Containers dropped like space junk
        On rolling bearings
        The foreshore has heard this all before
        Sandbags are fat and heavy
The riverbank has gobbled the crops and buried the dead

Helga Jermy

Previously published in *Australian Poetry Anthology 2016*

A Womb of Trees

After the exhibition 'The Long Game' by David Keeling, Dick Bett Gallery, 2016, paintings about Narawntapu National Park, Tasmania

'…there are realms where souls
crushed by the weight of the world
find refuge.'*

When you want to go back
tunnel into the trees, feel your body
soften, your mind clear, no need
to think, the caress of shadow, the cool relief,
curl back into the animal you once were
and before that, a speck of possibility
in the air, relive your pre-birth potential
when you drifted in a rich dark universe.
Listen to the whisper of the she-oaks, know
their poise, their fine needle-like foliage perfectly
segmented. Feel eternity, here, now. Delay
your departure towards the light
that shimmers blue, a vast ocean where
waters will break again and a cry will be heard
before the next rush of blinding reality.

Anne Collins

* From 'The Cadenced Roar of the Waves' by Rosalia de Castro

My Cliff Face Self

The weather is my veil
and inner mood, which passes
like hours on the glass my fine sand makes.
Water composes me
my eyes contain memories and streams
of half a thousand years.

Knock me over, break me, blow me away,
my rock face endures.
Birds
nestle
in my crevices,
till the morning sun lights up
my coloured layers.
The loving grip of lichen tattoos my skin
with hieroglyphs.
If you freeze my limbs,
they are still alive with vines.

The presence of owls
gives me courage,
multiplies my own sureness.
My ribbon sides scramble down
to meet the southern times
of settlement

where soft hills are mown green
by cattle.

Diana Bell Brooks

The Lambing, Night Watch

When moon and stag meet
in dark light snow quiet
fox cough
owl-hoot shadows
evening would hold its breath
scattered in rooks shout
blackbird night song
still as ear-ringing bells
brief as frosted air
faint exhalations drift
in the catch of torch-shine
slight the mist black comes
wind gentle as showers' touch
sharp as hedgerow blackberries,
picked on an impulse
only a lover would understand,
gathers fog into the valley
while yellow strings of afterbirth
cling warm to my fingers.

Peter Hansen

paranoid wind

Six weeks of you, wind.
You are drying out the world.
The stars have burnt and fallen
to the cracked mud floors of dams.
Logs block tracks, and daylight
sharpens shadows over stones.

Hungry for paranoid feed
I know it's you, wind, slamming doors,
swivelling leaves from silver eyes
to green sardonic smiles.
I won't jump or rattle.
Ruffle parrots. Hassle trees.

The animals concur:
we'll wait you out, and anyway
we are all being watched:
the spider by the wasp,
the lizard by the butcher-bird,
the eagle by the satellite

the man in the uniform
by his overseer, her overseer,
the watchers of the watchers,
the whisperers, and you, wind –
wind that sometimes howls
from the hidden mouths of trees.

Tim Metcalf

meteor shower

stars streak across
a night sky canvas
perforating the
picture perfect
scene

meteor shower
expected, yet unpredictable
each star minutes apart
like contractions
before a quixotic delivery

now perpendicular
now diagonal, slow
but quickening, like
the touch of a newborn
on the mother's face

synaptic flashes
as our planet braces
for more incursions
from space
a rebirth of intelligence
a reboot for the species perhaps

Fiona McIlroy

silence...

without sound
containing the hum
and hiss
of humanity;
the whisper or wild winds' roar;
the sussurating swoosh
of bird's wing
slicing silently
the profound nothing –
knowing all
containing all
and nothing
silently.
it is there
on the edge of the grand canyon,
in the shade
and sun of uluru;
it is in an english dale
and somewhere in my being
beyond the sometimes wild
beating of my heart;
beyond my thinking
and steady breaths,
but there –
silently

Jacqueline Lonsdale Cuerton

When winter winds blow

Wild is a word for the sea's lamentations
when westerly winds wreak grim devastation,

seething with venom on foam-splattered waves
that surge to the shore, over cliffs, into caves.

No safety, no shelter for fishing boats moored
at small wooden jetties now menaced, now gnawed

by pounding assaults on the pylons below
of a pulsating fury that will not let go.

Ashen-cloaked gulls ride the tide of the wind,
at times barely moving as they try to find

a crossbar that's safe on tall swaying masts
not sure if the hour is 10 to or 10 past.

In a world with no colour to brighten the view
their red beaks stand out, their yellow eyes too

reflect the wild world of a merciless coup
to all who would sail on this menacing brew.

Like a grey army blanket a glowering cover
of sky hunkers down and darkness now hovers

all over a world that was once summer mild,
and tells us there's months yet of winter's wind wild.

Jill Gloyne

Rainforest Fungi at Dusk

Lake Allom, Fraser Island, Queensland

A laggard lance of light
a flaccid lumen strand, a soaked spaghetti:
expelled from oceans resting on the canopy
extruded through the press of forest branches
exhausted as it fell like crashing feathers
now lit a tiny showcase in its bath.

In session run till night
for close-of-day performance to the gallery
an audience was simply immaterial
a matinee for none or many hundreds.
The artist with self-gratifying needs
displayed her gem beside Lake Allom's path.

Max Merckenschlager

Beyond the Tree of Heaven

I turn my back on the whitewashed stone cottage,
sniff drifting woodsmoke, imagine the iron kettle
singing softly on the stove behind the sound of voices
as Grandma Robinson talks with my mother.

I walk along the road and over the canal bridge,
push through green curtains of weeping willow,
inhale the sappy scent of Chinese Tree of Heaven
that grows wild on the common.

Between the canal bank and the wide river
1 find my secret place – the deep dark pool
left from when the flood came
after spring thaw in the mountains.

Lying flat on my belly,
I breathe in the coolness
of damp earth and new grass.
When river red gums' reflections break
and faint ripples spread in rings,
I focus my eyes on the tea-coloured water
where moving darker shapes tell me the platypus
is swimming with her young.

Robyn Mathison

Previously published in an earlier form in *Studio* #127

January seafarers

There's nothing wild about an early fog
as it settles smiling across the field
where green surrounds hay bales, golden backlog
of summer's long forgotten harvest yields.
Calm curtain with nothing of wild sea's grey haze
far distant where travellers battle winds
across the fury of last winter days
which settle on the lands which war transcends.
The fog which clouds the heads so dulled by pain
of others grasping straws lost high on wind,
new stories told to those who can retain
some trust when morning's graciousness has dimmed.
A calm conveying nothing of the minds
with hope anew, leaving wildness behind.

Adèle Ogiér Jones

Undersong

If there is sky,
if there is summer,
if the wild wind hides
and the sob through the pines has dulled
to a small wing's minor beat,
to a cricket's pulsing breath,
the day radiates the sibilance of eucalypt,
thin leaf edges turned to the sun.

And if rain veils the canopy,
weaves errant threads of timpani,
if sandstone drips staccato
and braided runnels lilt a rippled tone,
then the creek fattens,
sings soft arias.

We dare not move or speak,
hear undersongs we won't disturb,
believe we don't belong, think
all will vanish
like the puff of a fungus ball,
leaf shift, beetle click, seed split.

Shy ducklings rustle reeds,
our whispers peal like thunder.
We breathe too much.

Irene Wilkie

Previously published in *Poetry and Place Anthology 2015*, Close-Up Books

As Summer Comes

Last day of spring:
tawny husks of eucalypt leaves
cluster in dry gutters, toasted
by ultraviolet, desiccated by the westerly,
fire-fuel in a fretful world bearing down
with a season too anxious to be born.

Swiftly, jacaranda petals fall
and dust the concrete streets with regal hues.
Indigo clouds, above and below, hold storms
that threaten, but retreat, never able
to release their load of leaden moisture
that could mend the world.

The night between us is full
of dry heat and regretful longing.
Tawny husks of skin and gristle,
we hold ourselves apart
in a gully of long dreaming hours
and one last shared slumber.

Julie Thorndyke

of gales and zephyrs

birds and clouds must know its essence
might even know
where the wind comes from

constant gusting can sculpt the trees
create oceanic fleets of white horses
of hairdos, make havoc

of sand hills and history, dust
the southerly buster brings relief
a gentle breeze, solace

I've seen a roaring gale
lift waves to the top of high cliffs
off western Ireland

I've heard the Italian sirocco
can stir you crazy in a day
I've known of great gods of the air

messengers Hermes and Mercury in the west
creator Ehécatl in Mexico
but my grandmother had been dead fifty years

before I learned one of her sayings
about the chill blowing off the Canoblas
and I caught the myth of wind
from my own hometown

Jacqueline Buswell

underbelly

mountains cool, mist rolling down like thick sea spray, ferns, grottos, shafts of light, moss & lichen, muddy creeks, fig trees & cabbage palms tumbling down, escarpment meets sea, creek into lagoon lagoon into sea, plastic bags & bottles into creek into lagoon into sea, sands hot & gritty, waves cool & foamy, seaweedy, plasticy underbelly of the swell, waves breaking onto rocks pooling into crevices, crabs hard ochre shells barnacles creature & rock as one, bottles & bags floating…

Kathleen Bleakley

Previously published in *Azure*, Ginninderra Press Pocket Poets 61, 2017

Considering Fred Williams's Landscapes

Odd that we never
really noticed
how our trees look
straggling up a hillside,
ragged against the sky.
Until he showed us.

Farewell Claude and Constable,
Glover and Heysen too,
with your luxury
of form and light and shade,
noble trees and rolling cloud,
shining stream and the glow
of early evening…

No, we are set down
in amorphous scrub
on a scorching summer's day;
we are drenched in yellow ochre
scattered with what appear
to be random blobs of impasto.

Of course, there is light there
but it seems like
the unforgiving glare of noon.
Yet we could not be
more in this landscape.
Perhaps we'd always known
it in our bones – just needed him
to rip conditioning veils aside.

Barbara Fisher

Sunday at the Lake

so little movement
in the silent sparkling lake
this cool morning
no ball-mad ginger poodle
is plunging through the ripples

no wild splashing
no wavelets in her wake –
a swan appears
leading cygnets in peace
from shore to empty shore

there's a body
by the reeds a flat grey fish –
instinctively
I mouth the command 'leave it'
to a dog who isn't here

the heft and fire
of that aquatic creature
are light ashes now
settled in a ginger jar
at the lakeside home we shared

Amelia Fielden

Previously published in *Atlas Poetica*, Issue 22, 2017

A murmuration

On the wind a wing
of wave form in
elegant, organised flurry
contorting into the muscular dark
light on clouds
the shroud twisting DNA spiral miracles
that lift from the estuary,
from the sea

The grey salt water that
embodies their formless
and elusive, subverting
conscious mass,
ignition of air
torrent of wing
engulfing the mind
of eye bewildering
skewing and shaping
the very sky

A tumbling dance of life,
you fly
into the eye,
the collective eye of us all
beyond,
into maelstrom centres
of imagined birds,
that escape,
escape all earthly vision
and disappear.

Chris Hall

The moon is in its place
a crescent of gold…

missing is the majestic angophora,
limbs that nightly cradled the moon
to rest in ghostly arms and in drifts
of eucalypt scent shared secrets
of scribbled stories, carved on its skin.

Now only a smoking mast
in a sea of blackened wasteland.
Home to creatures great and small
winged, crawlers, furred, feathered,
the hairy, the hoofed woolly and wild.

All gone…
In the winds of change
the land will struggle to rise again,
as it has done before, in aeons past
and I will be looking for the moon.

ML Grace

Flexing

Mostly a restful blue-grey
Sun-sparkled river of light
Forming a backdrop to our lives
The tidal reach sometimes flexes
Its strength

We watched all afternoon
As a king tide
Pushed the waters
Higher and higher
Till the posts where the pelicans sit
Were almost covered

By evening all tranquillity was gone
Like a hungry animal
Dull turgid water
With swirls of litter-filled
Brown-stained froth
Lapped at the rocks
And in some places
Clawed its way over the path

Energy spent the tide turned
Meekly the waters dropped
Slinking off out to sea
Leaving us with human detritus
And a disquiet about what might happen
With global warming

Brenda Eldridge

Winter

It's no use
blaming
the crumpled foil sea
or the passive
dark clouds hung low.

You lost your colours
long before this grey day.
See how the curious bird
points its yellow eye
in your direction? Look

at the way it spreads its wings
then lifts
legs trailing
and marks itself stark-white
between sea and sky.

Angela Johnson

Antipodes

It was to the sun that she had given herself,
That ancient topaz god.
Brazenly yielding,
Bronzed and ablaze
Bearing honey-eyed offspring.
Light-footed, airily springing
Fecund valleys,
Blue-boned mountains
And quartzy glister streams.
They bounded and bloomed.

But, beyond the zaffre seas
The crust of salt stained sails bore down upon her
As though she were some glistening whore.

Oaken-chested, dry-eyed men tilted their mettle and smoked her horizons,
Swaggering at her damascene shoreline, yellowing her white petticoats to shreds.
They hollowed out her forests and spread her ice so thin.

They supped amongst the visceral squalor of her entrails and didn't stop to wonder what it meant.

As clay formed upon her cicatrices they parcelled up strips of her and shipped it away.
But returned to scour her gold-slashed veins.

In his fire and fury the sun moved closer,
His molted eyes glaring and his might closing in on their frail winter.
And the men cooled themselves at the shrivelling sea and shaded their eyes,
Because they knew no better.

Jane Carmody

moreton bay fig

she must be more than a century,
no longer concerned
with appearances,
gnarled roots exposed,
wrinkled trunk, limbs
tangling skyward with
crows perched in
her green rinse

she's cantankerous – dropping
fruit over neighbour's fences,
and secretive, whispering in
the ears of the children
who play beneath

her scent is always earthy
and over-ripe, having long
given up on seasons
but not on life

Kevin Gillam

Rough Sea Journey

Port Grimaud to St Tropez

The sea, from the hotel balcony,
has changed to angry white flecks on grey.
Gone, its gentle vibe of the last few days,
a strong wind carelessly tossing a beach chair,
cans and other rubbish across the sand.

We drive to the harbour
and board the ferry for St Tropez,
seawater slopping loudly against the timbers.
Out into the open sea, troughs form
rocking us violently from side to side,
water surging across the deck, soaking passengers.

The ocean is black, its rough waves send us riding high
before dragging us back down into a channel
then up, lurching down, again and again
battering us against each other as we struggle
to keep our balance, heavy spray lashing the windows
our knuckles white on the seat in front.

In the distance, I see a lonely yacht
being buffeted high, then dropping back
into a trough so deep
only the mast is visible
and I wonder how it can survive.

After an eternity
we splutter the last few metres to the jetty
clamber wobbly-legged up the ferry ramp
thankful to step on dry land.

Jill Gower

Gum Saplings

Like running paint
    or dripping teabags,
        their bark is brown on pale.
            They're like skewbald horses
                galloping along a grassy skyline.
                Tall and pencil-like;
                    they're a knocked-over
                        box of Derwents.

Jayne Linke

Paterson's Curse

Echium plantagineum

I look down as the plane begins its gradual descent to Wagga;
winter rains have put an end to drought across the Riverina.
Shining veins of watercourses mime the lupin blue of sky;
water meadows advertise their amplitude with glancing light.

Fields of colour ramify; emerald, loam-brown, russet, gold;
chrome-yellow canola; amethyst the eyes emulsify.
Beside the road beyond the town, the amethyst grows more intense –
gentian violet trumpets on a minor scale ascend tough stems,

armed with barbs of cilia as self-defence. Do the barbs enable insects –
like a ladder – or impale them? If a horse or cow feasts on these flowers,
it will die. Yet the plant relies on animals dispersing seed.
Can kangaroos resist its toxins, though it's not a native weed?

Do the bees, preferring blue dyes to all other floral pigments,
work this pollen into tainted honey that subdues the hive?
The iris hue evokes the innocence of childhood; morning glory;
the secret formula in laundry knobs of Reckitt's Blue.

Later, it's a memory cue for the Arles I briefly knew,
revisited through van Gogh's vision: cobalt; starry indigo.
Despite the slow demise they bring to wasting livestock, cursed by farmers,
trumpet-florets of this noxious weed are harbingers of spring.

Jena Woodhouse

Published in *New Shoots Poetry Anthology*, The Red Room Company, 2017

Winter Beach

For Brenda

An elemental brotherhood
of sand, ocean, wind,
forms a heaving sea surface
ready for attack on the passive shore.

Like predators
confronting their prey,
waves encircle the
stalwart stanchions
under the jetty
– sentinels on guard.

With majestic energy
Poseidon rises,
and the grating roar
of pebbles beneath his feet,
sounds like a furious
army on the move.

Howling winds befriend
tiered rows of white horses
hurling one upon the other,
until breathless,
with the joy of possession,
they bolt to the beach.

Rose Helen Mitchell

Close your eyes

A dead-leaf covered floor
cracks with each step.
A dull light lingers
in the space between
two low-lying branches
while bright little speckles
form above a canopy
of jagged limbs.

The evening is hot
and even the crickets are quiet
as the moon finds its place
above a violet horizon.
Voices echo through the trees
calling out to our dying hearts.

Jeff A. Harbrow

The Ancient Guardians

linger in this place
behind a splash of sunlight, never sighted
darkling amongst shadows…

When swollen, the rivulet twinkles rapidly
its joyous abundant dance singing
from rocks and eddies, or
as she dwindles into brown occasional pools,

having left the world of form and matter
They reside in the *Timeless* – listening.

Does an ant bite deep into a toe?
Do blackberries entwine your clothing?
Beware lest you chance to stumble!

Past wrongs are not forgotten as
our fleeting, shifting world moves on. What
we indifferent folk ignore, *They* recall:
       slaughter and rapine of an ancient race.

As I grow my foreign vegetables, plant northern bulbs,
reflective *They* glance with tolerant awareness
Always *They* watch – and always *They* remember…

One day will come their reckoning.

Jen Gibson

Telling the Wild Wood Story

Gentlemanly Ratty,
old Badger in his den,
dear rustic Mole –
no wildness in them;
but in the Wild Wood –
what then?
Myth and fear,
mysteries held dear;
there were… 'No
not DRAGONS, silly.
Listen!'
There were
sharp-eyed ferrets
with spiteful stare,
weasels with
their cunning air
and stoats – oh dear,
most unrefined…
they made THAT clear!
So, with their cries
and eerie whistles,
they spread their threats
among the thistles.
They gave the wood
its Wild Wood name yet
Badger lived there
just…the…same!
Now Moley was bored
and crept off to see
the wicked Wild Wood – oh lord!…

Jan Norman

Different Every time

A shore, some days a dream,
        silver fish torpedo
through transient glass

and whales in the bay,
        some days pounding in
driven by the lows that fury this coast

or bright with waves that come again and again
        and again so you can barely lungful
before the next.

A plastic lighter in the sand –
        thank god it doesn't work
that'd be too poetic – fire from waters

and a drowned Prometheus further along
        a sodden letter tucked into orange overalls
sea bloat, face down, crows already –

no, just lovers lean the wind
        looking for a place in this wildness
before the rain.

Peter Frankis

Lone tree silhouette

Poised atop a high hill
        best viewed from a moving vehicle
    always in relationship with its own special light
it makes its stand
        capturing and fastening to itself
                for the brief duration
                      the viewer's gaze
a solitary tree

This no great giant
        straining huge limbs
                towards the sky

Discarding the company of others
        it flaunts its courageous fragility
                exulting in its defiant isolation
It bares for all its delicate structure
        sculptured by the most sensitive creator
Such distance deceives the viewer
        but its skeletal appearance is misleading
Those limbs are fuelled by vitality
a genuine majesty results

Now it is gone
        disappeared from view
But never gone
        the viewer uplifted
    after such a communion

Greg Tome

Winter Storm Front

North-west Tasmania

Icy Antarctic blasts
sweep across the island
trees bent, an agony of twisted limbs
swirling leaves jettisoned on air
birds shriek out alarms
clawing, clinging to footholds

All melds into a frenzy
senses confused
colours, sounds, smells overlap

Ocean churns and froths
erupting against the sky
as horizontal rain slants in
whipping along streets
roofs clattering
a million cutting knives

Heavy clouds of dark grey sails
fill the sky
rudderless, surging forwards
an armada threatening
no quarter given in any direction

Thérèse Corfiatis

The Weight of Water

The Yarra Yarra, last river I swam, back when I thought it fun
to burden our ancient Honda with polyethylene hulls.
In Bellbird Park we would struggle into neoprene wetsuits,
boots and gloves, unload the kayaks and drag them through mud.

A day's work before we could pass beneath the filmic suspense
of two hundred thousand fruit bats. Your disgust
when I, slathered scalp to sole with E. coli, said I'd sooner drink
urine than sip one drop of this. The care with which we put

our lips to Boathouse caffè lattes. The current insists.
Irresistible force brought to bear by a fall of only inches,
the boat rolls, spills the occupant, me, among green-coiffed boulders.
To try and stand, to resist the flow, risks an ankle caught and twisted,

or worse, a slip, head struck on stone, to lie prone,
ceding vital heat to indifferent shallows. The image stuck.
We stopped going. Then came the day a helicopter drummed
a little Christian lost, news of the child searched for

and found, succumbed to a love of flowing water,
mere metres from home, his pyjama-clad form among fallen leaves,
surface scum and suspended debris. The tree shading
where he stumbled now a shrine – nursery version

of those roadside crosses – hung with shiny stars and suns,
fading fairies and a unicorn with wings.
Averse to the wild, we scuttled our losses,
never bought the things we could've worn.

J. Richard Wrigley

Previously published in a differently edited form in 'The End', the 2017 edition of *Visible Ink*

'The wild begins where you least expect it,
one step off your normal course.'

Bernard Malamud

Invasion

Music and Poetry are feral beasts;
they prowl dark forests underneath the moon
sliding through shadows dangerous and deep
wrapped in the shawls and fringes of the night;
they saunter silently to hidden pools
to bend their mighty heads and softly lap
scattering droplets in a silver stream;
they yawn and stretch and writhe their bodies round
in mystic circles, claim their dreaming place
and slumber under eiderdowns of stars.

Obsessed with them, their beauty and their grace,
you hunt them through the unforgiving day
and into evening where the twilight fades,
seeking to catch a glimpse of glowing eyes
or sniff their musky perfume on the breeze.
For such magnificence, you'd risk your life
and so you follow deep between the trees
to watch and listen, curb your thundering heart
and offer up your throat to claws and teeth.

You cannot tame them, but they make their choice,
accept your worship as their proper due,
and if you keep the faith and stand your ground
they'll slink in through the catflap of your mind
explore the corners of your deepest dreams
and curl up on the hearthrug of your soul.

Mary Jones

Previously published in *Second Person Singular*, Ginninderra Press Pocket Poets 42, 2016

The black one

And later, when my life is winding down,
when the possible has become improbable,
and the facts of my little life
are heading fast for a gathering of daisies
and a dash between two dates,
there'll be this:

a Sunday afternoon,
me marking spelling tests;
my son, hungover,
sprawled in front of the television
watching as an oil slick of wildebeests
ten miles long, winds its way to the river.

He, ignoring the crocodiles bibbing up
for breakfast, the fragility of life,
the certain threat of it all ending badly,
turning to me, smiling and saying,
'Mum, out of all those wildebeests,
which one do you like the best?'

Louise Nicholas

A matter of perspective

Ambiguous, that word, wild.

Wildflowers in the countryside –
beautiful indeed.
Innocent, unspoiled and lovely.
Growing free, untrammelled,
unconfined.

But walk along a city street,
noting, with a disapproving glance,
how wild your neighbour's garden,
its weeds undisciplined,
rampant, where you want control.

Leave animals to roam in jungles;
wild things should not be prisoners.
So cruel to shut them up in zoos.
Open doors of cages; let birds
return to freedom of the air.

But keep your dogs chained;
walk them leashed, sedately,
along the beach. Too wild
to risk near children.

The charms of freedom,
spontaneity, have real allure –
but how much wildness
do we really want?

Valerie Volk

Flux

Feral is the weed that walks, hops or swims,
that we seeded here first of all.
Like weapons in Afghanistan to fight the Russians,
they shoot back against the giver, given time.
The irony in the soil, the punchline
that keeps moving.
They are the spoonful of toad that never
helped the sugar.

The feral is the new devil;
we burn them, use their live bodies for cricket,
run them over with gleeful cars.
They are our scapegoats, scapetoads, scapecarp,
whipping boys for our royal, stupid selves.

Varmint, pest, pets gone wild, rejigged –
dancing to their own tune.

PS Cottier

Previously published (as 'Feral') on pscottier.com, in March 2017

Spoken Words

Feverish with poetry
Spitting tortured rhymes
Into the faded mesh of a microphone
Hoping to flush wild words away.

On the out-breath
Of unspoken voices
Amplified chaos
Traces of our stories
Become more bearable
Soothing the sensation
That we are barely here at all
Even if we only show up
Inside a lonely moment on stage
Oscillating between heartbreak
And justifiable rage
Even if we only expel
Truncated versions of our pain
When we speak about others
We speak of our own resilience
We replay and reframe
Narratives that would claim us
Captives of silence and shame.

Voluntarily we stand in front
Of others courageously
Feverish with poetry
Spitting tortured rhymes
Into the faded mesh of a microphone
Hoping to flush wild words away.

Gabrielle Journey Jones

Moonlit Beauty

It gripped my throat
and sprang into my chest
a gasping breath of wonder.

Mesmerised I watched
the beauty of liquid moonlight
slide off her lithe body
of scales and pearlescent skin.

High in the air she flipped
a backwards arc
drops of water flinging wide
oblivious in her freedom.

My yearning rose and disappeared
with her under the waves.

Alone now I lay in my pool
a golden chain tethering my tail
captive to that wonder
and
no longer fully tame.

Susan Fitzgerald

Riparian Zone

The road was empty that evening
the last one

all I could see were those eyes
a white tiger's penetrating blue
your wildness held in check

shouts from the shore
the band played loudly
we thought, for a New York minute
that it was a celebration
but it was just a diversion
two paths diverging
each leading nowhere
winding as DNA, a double helix
twist back to the start

there's a whisper in the forest
that outdoes the trumpets
whippoorwills, nightjars singing
the softest most mournful whistle
invisible as their bodies
hidden in foliage
it's still there if you focus

a corruption of politicians
in diminishing returns
the indelible burn of footsteps
on soft plants
a riparian zone from the past.

Magdalena Ball

Bronte Beach

The surf's been hammered by rain,
and along the pavement open-faced cafés wedge side by side:
compact, glass-fronted, in flattened
Art Deco buildings, with competing blackboard menus.
Rain drips from the edge of the canvas awning,
and a smell of fried fish in rancid oil
through the mouth of the sliding door
as an oversized bus pulls in and blocks the view.
Marooned on the swell are wetsuited board riders,
unwavering as the cliff face above the rocks that define the beach.
Beyond the rock pool the waves
remain stubbornly low spreading a shallow calm.
The rain settles, rusting roof racks in the salt air,
and those expired meters will upset the fattened
people-who-lunch in the darkening afternoon.
All day the treacherous ocean scours
the man-made sea pool, where
all-weather swimmers scan the water
for migrating dolphins or whales.
A white-hulled speedboat appears
in the grey-blue, travelling north,
and the black-clad board riders wait,
grounded, legless pigeons who can,
in a heartbeat, fan their iridescent wings.
Squabbling seagulls swoop and dive
and chase each other between the palms,
each white slow and steady flap of wings
picked up by the whiteness of the backwash
of the speed boat out there on the pastel-pink ocean,
disappearing behind the haze.

Libby Sommer

Free within the Cage

Thrashing
In the cobwebs of convention
Bound by ties
Of one's own design
Shackled by trends
And frameworks, necessary for survival.

An unreleased demo
A hidden, unfinished track
True purpose blunted
Potential kept in check
A wild thing pruned
Pressure to complete
What has barely begun
A blossoming artwork
Stifled by a frame too small
If only the locale were different
If only the circumstances were altered
If only it were another age
How the song may play
With alternate instruments.

These are the limiters
All that remains
Is an undisclosed period of time
In order to adapt.

Anthony J. Langford

Stampede

A spark disturbs the leaf litter
    of a dawning brain;
it smoulders and smokes
    the semi-consciousness;
ignites imagination with
    increasing intensity
setting to furious flight
    a surge of words
disorganised and entangled like
    panicking beasts
following instinct to chaos
    in fleeing a wild forest fire.

From the crackling canopy
    they dash and dart
in haphazard unpredictability
    racing and spacing
from crowded crush
    to dispersed individuals:
a continuum of confusion
    unified in urgency;
the fierce and the meek
    gallop, stagger, scurry
in a unit of desperation
    all seeking safe destination.

The law of natural selection
    decides death or survival.
Exhausted, the fittest only
    finally fall in repose on the page.

Dianne Kennedy

Safety in numbers

there they are now, this latest mob –
thirteen –
between black stumps, down on that flat
with young at foot
under this sunset so warm
by the creek running dry
such great beasts fully grown
grazing in what they call pasture
that we see just as grass…just as ours

their red-white tails swishing at flies
as one
they browse, chewing cud on the side
with feet called hooves
turning soil to mud so thick
across that shallow ford
fouling a stream once clear
no eye out for danger themselves
certain about safety in numbers

as for those of us left up here –
just three –
behind ringbarked trees, on this rise
all we can do
despite a sundown so pink
is to sniff at the breeze
for gunshot armpit scents
in what our people call country
pouches empty as we bound away

Rodney Williams

Old Vinyl Anger

Shame on you!
One and all.
My family – who I suffered for
each time you sat
your rumps on me
through many years.

When new, you
hummed and hawed.
Le Cornus. Good price too.
Not leather, vinyl.
Was cheaper, lasted years.

Then, on a whim, you
bought another. Stripped
me to my bareness. Gutted.
Cut in two. Ripped open.
Unloved. Abandoned.
Dumped here – forgotten.

Where gone the hearts
I nurtured young
and in my prime? My fate
uncertain – loved only
by coarse weeds
that thrust so wildly
up my arse.

Martin Christmas

The Lie

This day is solely a pretence
to a lucid illusion gone awry
a fabricated reality,
with enough truth to believe in the lie.
We are under the influence
of a system that was built to evolve,
leaving our mindsets paralysed,
to believe in a pure lack of resolve.

For we have unknowingly slipped
towards injustice and oppression,
but what's this day without the past,
and our capacity for regression?
So let's disregard what was taught,
for knowledge is power to the founder.
We'll go primitive once again
and then watch the authorities flounder.

Andrew Drake

Water World

On New Year's Eve or some other wildly
Arbitrary celebration, looking over the wold
From fifty metres up at Wet and Wild
While children dive into wave-wielding,

> I get a text. It is part of a letter
> From Marianne Moore to Elizabeth Bishop,
> 'One of the most beautiful things
> I have ever seen at the movies,'

Plunging down the switchback like wildebeest
Crossing in thousands the water whorled
And treacherous, the children greet the water world
With wails of delight waylaid.

> 'An alligator farm in Alabama –
> Alligators ascend an artificial bluff
> To chute the chute and slide down
> Only to toil up to do it again.'

No more beautiful use of the wild word
Than Keats' on first looking into the weald
Just as Cortez and his men mild-willed
Looked at each other with a wild surmise.

John Watson

The Kettle Boils

A rondeau

The kettle boils and lets off steam;
enraged, I sometimes want to scream!
The neighbourhood can hear me roar
as I walk out and slam the door.
My patience lost, my ire's extreme.

Beware! My eyes will start to gleam –
A warning sign – a laser beam
That penetrates your very core.
The kettle boils!

But this is not what it might seem.
It's my own faults I would redeem,
It's with myself I'm feeling sore.
A cup of tea will soon restore
the balance of my self-esteem.
The kettle boils!

Antony Fawcus

A Holy Night – By Way of Explanation

The cartoonist thought it easy to be happy
and the patient asked why he was most often sad.

Morning rain saturated the canvas chairs
on the breakfast terrace; and a late sun
shone hard till they dried.

The new house creaked and snapped
with growing pains; and an old oak
groaned as it met once more with wind.

A willy wagtail turned east to west
in an eyeblink; yet the duck was forever
far from the pond.

Stars clustered, soared and arranged the
constellation of the Southern Cross;
and our wild thunderstorm brought lightning.

The pillows on the bed were soft
and some hard, whilst day into night

was an upward movement – the ground
more dark than a newly expired match.

Rebecca Kylie Law

Exit from the City

leaving La Trobe Street
as the late afternoon
sunlight is muzzled by shadow

everywhere
the muffled grunt of traffic
is fast forwarding

eager as sleigh-dogs
office workers are bursting
out of elevators and onto streets

along Victoria Parade
an endless print run of leaves
are falling with the same regularity
as commuters gathering at tram stops

from every orifice of the city
the peak hour rush is oozing out
making the city less sizeable

vehicles are following each other
along the same worn trade routes
to the suburbs

on Elizabeth Street a woman
slices her way across six lanes of traffic

her bike spins as recklessly
as roulette wheels

Jules Leigh Koch

Afterword

When I first thought of the theme Wild for a new poetry collection to celebrate the tenth anniversary of Ginninderra Press's relocation to Port Adelaide, I hoped, with more wishfulness than certainty, that Ginninderra Press poets across Australia would respond to the richly diverse range of subjects and approaches that I thought the theme might suggest – wild animals and birds inevitably, wild environments of course, wild weather as you'd expect, but wild people and wild behaviour too, in both positive and negative guises.

As poems started to come in, which they did very quickly and, as this book shows, in extraordinary numbers, my hopes resolved into deep satisfaction. Over 150 Ginninderra Press poets – some well known, some whose first-ever poem appears within theses pages – did 'get it'. And by some creative miracle, scarcely any two poets turned out to have written about the same aspect of the theme. Even when the inspiration was the same creature or a similar event, or the same facet of behaviour, or the shared experience of wilderness writ large, the resulting poems were always very different.

Then, in the hands of Joan Fenney, who had the task of deciding which poems were in and which were not, a cohesive (you could almost say *un*wild!) shape emerged, resulting in the book you're holding in your hands.

I couldn't be prouder of this book and its contributors. It's a brilliant marker of another milestone in the life of Ginninderra Press.

Stephen Matthews

www.ingramcontent.com/pod-product-compliance
Lightning Source LLC
Chambersburg PA
CBHW071843080526
44589CB00012B/1094